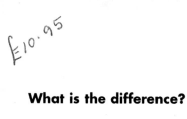
What is the difference?

Withdrawn

What is the difference?

A new critique of adult learning and teaching

Alan Rogers

niace
promoting adult learning

Published by the National Institute of Adult
Continuing Education (England and Wales)
Renaissance House, 20 Princess Road West
Leicester LE1 6TP

Company registration no: 2603322
Charity registration no: 1002775

First published 2003, reprinted 2004, 2006

promoting adult learning

NIACE has a broad remit to promote lifelong learning opportunities
for adults. NIACE works to develop increased participation in
education and training, particularly for those who do not have
easy access because of barriers of class, gender, age, race, language
and culture, learning difficulties and disabilities, or insufficient financial
resources.

For a full catalogue of NIACE's publications, please visit
http://www.niace.org.uk/publications

Cataloguing in Publications Data
A CIP record for this title is available from the British Library

ISBN 10: 1 86201 184 2
ISBN 13: 978 1 86201 184 7

Cover design by: Creative Associates, Oxford
Designed and typeset by: Newgen Imaging Systems (P) Ltd. Chennai, India
Printed and bound in Great Britain by Lightning Source, Milton Keynes

Contents

Foreword

This small book grew out of a series of discussions on adult learning held at the Center for International Education in the University of Massachusetts early in 1999 during a six-month sabbatical I spent there. Its thesis has been tested out in a number of seminars given at postgraduate level in several different universities over the past three years. I am very grateful to the academics and students with whom I interacted during that pleasant stay and the subsequent seminars.

The argument presented here is a development of my research in the 1980s – in part a recantation and in part a progression, further steps in the journey I am undertaking. It contains an elaboration of the argument which I have outlined in successive editions of *Teaching Adults* (Rogers 1986, 1996 and 2002). In that book, I suggested that if we wish to be effective in the way we teach adults, we need to understand and build upon the natural learning practices and processes that adults employ in what I called 'learning episodes'. I believe this even more strongly now than I did at the first time of writing and I have spent a good deal of time since then exploring what those natural learning practices and processes are. What is presented here is a summary of those studies.

This book, I believe, contains a distinctive approach to understanding adult learning. It is in large part rooted in what many others have had to say earlier. A great deal has been written about adult learning, especially in the last few years as the orthodoxy of 'lifelong learning/education' has taken root in so many different countries. Much rethinking has taken place and is taking place, although the scene is still confused. I see this short study as making yet one more contribution to the growing appreciation of adult learning, one which will affect what educational planners will plan and what teachers of adults will do. It will lead on, I hope, to ever more clarity and increased effectiveness.

Alan Rogers
Uppingham, January 2003

Introduction

The question at issue

The question which has plagued many educators for generations and which we attempted to deal with in detail in the 1970s and 1980s is this: Is adult education different from children's education? That question still faces us today; thus we can still ask whether "adulthood as a time of life brings with it a way of learning (and a corresponding set of practices for facilitating this learning) that is not paralleled at earlier stages of the lifespan" (Brookfield 2000: 89). Important practical and policy issues flow from the answer we give to that question.

Why revisit the question now?

There are, I think, a number of reasons for revisiting this question at this time. The first is the general movement from certainty to uncertainty which we all are experiencing. In the 1970s and 1980s, we were very sure that adult learning was different and therefore that adult teaching was different from younger persons' learning and teaching. Writers like Knowles, Knox, Kolb, Pat Cross and WA Chickering, to cite but a few, wrote extensively about the uniqueness of adults as learners from so many different perspectives. Perhaps the reason for this emphasis on the special nature of adult learning lay in the fact that adult education was at that time marginalised and unpopular with policy-makers. In the UK it had a weak statutory basis, unlike schools, higher education and further education. We found ourselves needing to stress the essentially distinctive nature of our work in order to establish our credentials as professional elements within the educational sector. There were also practical reasons: I, like others in the field, discovered that when teachers from other sectors of the educational world came to teach adults, they often found themselves using what both they and we felt were inappropriate methodologies and approaches; so that we all felt that teaching adults in practice was very different. As I said in the first edition of my earlier book, there was some confusion between what was distinctive about teaching adults and what was general good practice in all educational contexts (student-centred and active teaching-learning methods etc.). Nevertheless, we believed that at heart there was a fundamental difference about adult learning which we could (and indeed often did) set out in terms of a dichotomy.

Today, paradoxically at a time when the position of adult educators is more firmly established in policy terms than it has ever been, we are much less certain. There has been a spate of studies of learning, including adult learning, which have challenged every aspect of what we used to believe (see, for example, Merriam and Caffarella 1999; Sutherland 1997). Most of the orthodoxies have been challenged in one way or another (Kerka 2002; St Clair 2002). Much of this has been theoretical with (as Courtney and his colleagues have pointed out) relatively little empirical evidence to support the claims made (Courtney *et al.* 1999). But despite all this writing, there is much greater uncertainty today than ever before. We increasingly doubt, for example, whether it is possible to genericise adults – to assume that all adults are the same and behave/learn in the same distinctive way from all children, who are often similarly treated in a generic fashion (Tice 1997). We are uncertain about universal lifespan stages, about the applicability of learning styles to all people, about the effect different cultures will have on the constructs of learning and education. We are today much more aware of the diversity of the human race than ever before.

Secondly, much (but not all) of this rethinking has been caused by the upsurge of the concept and language of lifelong learning. The discourse of lifelong learning or lifelong education, suddenly and so widely accepted today, has led to many changes in the provision of learning opportunities for adults. In particular, it has resulted in practice in the opening up of formal educational institutions to what are called 'non-traditional students' (i.e. adult students) and to the introduction of formalised learning programmes into new venues such as the workplace (see, for example, Aspin *et al.* 2001; Longworth and Davies 1996; Sutherland 1997; Smith and Spurling 1999). The key element of the 'new educational order' in many countries seems to be the presence of 'adult' students in higher and further education – and that has inevitably raised the question among practitioners: In what ways is the teaching of adults different from the teaching of younger age students?

The third element in the need to revisit this question is the work that has been done in other but cognate fields of study. As we shall see, recent work on discourse analysis, post-colonialism, identity or identities, and on consciousness have all suggested new ways of thinking about adulthood and learning. They have certainly influenced my thinking and that of many others. It seems important to review what we once believed in the light of such new approaches, necessitating the question: In the light of all this study, can we say that adult learning and the teaching of adults are the same or different from those of younger persons? This is the focus of our search. I am not claiming this work as a piece of field-based research but an attempt to rethink the questions being asked in the light of other studies in cognate areas.

However, this question is in fact two questions, as Brookfield (2000) recognises, not just one – two questions of a rather different nature from each other. For, as we shall see, learning and education are not exactly the same, although they are closely related. Thus we need to rephrase the question in two different forms:

(a) Are the learning processes of adults and younger persons different or the same?

(b) In what ways are the various processes involved in the teaching of adults and younger persons different or the same? Or, perhaps we should rephrase it to ask: In what ways *should* the various processes involved in teaching adults and teaching younger persons be different or the same?

Even if we were to answer 'no' to the first question, it may be possible that teaching adults is or should be different for quite different reasons.

Learning and education/teaching

I start from the position that not only can we distinguish between learning and education, but we simply must. A great deal of the discourse of lifelong learning confuses the two. There are many writers today characterised by "the persistent confusion of education with learning" (Duke 2001: 502).

I appreciate the reasons why so many writers wish to get away from using the term 'education' and replace it with 'learning'. They see education as being equated with schooling, and they wish to stress that the main emphasis even in education is on learning. However, this language, in which learning and education "without justification being offered…have been collapsed into one" (Cohen and Leicester 2000: 74) is not only confusing; it is now recognised as being positively harmful. Throughout two recent and authoritative collections of statements on lifelong education (Field and Leicester 2000; Aspin *et al.* 2001), for example, there is a constant stress on the fact that education and learning are not the same, and that a distinction needs to be drawn even within the discourse of lifelong learning, that it is necessary "to emphasise lifelong *education* (rather than simply *learning*)" (Barrow and Keeney 2001: 60, original emphasis).

Of course, education and learning are inextricably connected, but just as flour and bread are related though not all flour is bread, so education and learning are related. Education must always include learning but not all learning is education; education is moulded out of learning by some agency. I want to suggest that an all-embracing definition of education is that it consists of a process of 'someone helping someone else to learn'. The discourse I shall adopt is one which sees education not simply as a system but as a process; which sees the educational system as designed or intended to bring about that process; and which believes that in so far as it fails to do that, the educational system ceases to be 'education'.

Such a definition provides the basis for a working distinction between learning and education. Education is assisted and purposeful learning, but there is also learning which is not educational. The view that "all events in which one is consciously involved throughout one's lifespan constitute education (as process) and contribute to and are part of one's education (as outcome)" is rejected here and by others on the grounds that it fails "to accord any intelligibility to the notion of formal and active engagement in educating activities as opposed to informal and unintentional [learning]" (Aspin and Chapman 2001: 13–14).

We therefore need to look at learning and at teaching/education separately. The first part of this book will be devoted to looking at learning and some implications for teaching, for I strongly believe we need to understand what it is if we are to promote learning in our teaching. The second part will examine education, which I define as any process designed to help others to learn (i.e. it is much wider than simply schooling) whether through face-to-face contact in classes or one-to-one, or through less formal means such as books and journals, etc. Throughout, we shall try to assess whether learning and teaching are the same processes for adults as for younger persons, and if they are different, then in what way.

Part I

Learning and adults

In this section, after looking at what is meant by learning, I argue that rather than one single all-embracing learning theory, there are in fact two distinct kinds of learning which I label 'task-conscious learning' and 'learning-conscious learning'; that these two types of learning are not restricted to adults and to younger persons exclusively but that both types of learning are engaged in by both younger persons and adults. This section also suggests that there is nothing distinctive about the kind of learning undertaken by adults, but that both kinds of learning can usefully be brought together in different mixes in order to create the most effective kind of learning for both groups of learners.

The nature of learning

Elsewhere, I have defined learning as changes in knowledge, understanding, skills and attitudes which lead to "those more or less permanent changes and reinforcements brought about... in one's patterns of acting, thinking and/or feeling" (Rogers 2002: 86). Such a definition seems to be generally agreed, but beyond this we enter a minefield of contested views about learning, whether in childhood or in adulthood.

I start from the position that we all learn all the time. "As human beings... we are a learning species" (Dixon 1999: 39). This is (as we have already noted) denied by many writers on lifelong learning. Their discourse speaks of people turning to learning, or yearning for learning (Longworth and Davies 1996). They talk of finding time, space and money for learning, as if learning was some special activity which only some people do (Smith and Spurling 1999). Various recent publications have reported that "almost one in four [persons] is currently learning" (the rest are not, apparently), that "more men than women participate in learning"; they speak of "people who have done no learning since leaving school", of "non-participation of adults in learning [because] people don't know where to go to find out about courses" (see Rogers 1997: 116)[1].

This last quotation indicates the problem. 'Learning' here is equated with 'learning opportunities', with 'planned learning events', with provision of various kinds, both in a classroom and outside of it. But there is all the other learning which people do in the course of living – learning by going to a football match or a concert, watching television or reading a newspaper, talking in a pub or going on holiday, getting married, buying a house and having a baby. There is the learning arising from the pursuit of hobbies and special interests. By speaking of those who have done no learning since leaving school (highly unlikely even in their own terms: what about learning to drive a car?), such writers ignore and in fact actively demean all the natural learning we all do all the time. They are

---

[1] Learning thus becomes 'courses': cf. a recent article headed 'Off the booze and into learning', where the text shows that 'learning' here means training, i.e. Supported training for alcohol rehabilitation, *Adults Learning* **13** (9): 12.

saying in effect that such learning is unimportant, that the only learning which counts is the kind of learning opportunities which they are talking about. "Hopeless confusion arises from indiscriminately swapping around the words 'education' and 'learning' " (Duke 2001: 508).

The whole purpose of this book is to try to redress the balance; to suggest that the natural learning we all do during the course of living is the most important kind, and that unless we understand and value it, we will never create effective learning opportunities for those we are so keen to get into such programmes. I repeat: all of us learn all the time; we are never away from learning. This is the most important thing that the discourse of lifelong learning has reminded us of – that learning is inevitably embedded within daily life, that our everyday experiences bring with them continuous learning.

This carries with it several important implications. First, there is no such person as a non-learner. Everyone is engaged in learning. They may not be learning what we want them to learn (so they may be away from *our* learning), but they are all learning. It is not helpful to use terms such as 'non-learner', or to confine the use of the term 'learner' to those who are in fact 'participants' (a perfectly good word for what is often meant by the word 'learner'). Non-participants are not non-learners. Secondly, learning is a natural process like breathing. One writer suggests it is a basic drive like sex (Walker 2001: 627), but I prefer the analogy with breathing (see also Jarvis *et al*. 1998: 1). Just as we all breathe but much of the time we are not conscious of it, so we all learn, even though at times we are not conscious of so doing.

Learning, then, is the way we relate to our experiences – the way such experiences change us and the way we try to change our experiences and make sense of them. Our experiences also extend to our leisure time as well as to our work time; to our social roles and cultural life as well as to our professional roles. It is a mixture of both proactive and responsive engagement with our lifeworld, "the process whereby knowledge is created through the transformation of experience" (Kolb 1984). Visser (2001: 453–4) speaks of learning as being dialogic (that is, we question our experience) and ecological (that is, it draws on the whole of our environment).

I suggest that we learn as our life changes. The many changes which life brings to all persons in all cultures provide both challenges and opportunities for learning. We can for convenience identify these changes in three ways:

(a) Our *social contexts* change; as we go through life, we enter many different roles, and society helps us to interpret those roles differently. Many of us become parents; but as we get older, we will interpret our roles as parent in relation to our children very differently (see below for more on roles). Our cultural contexts which help to form our identities are changing and every new role we enter and every new interpretation of these roles we adopt willingly or unwillingly will bring with it learning.

(b) Our *occupation* (not, please, our jobs: the dominance of the work discourse is very great at the moment. Caring in the home is as much an occupation as going out to work) will create many demands for learning; and we will actively create new perceptions of ourselves within those occupations as time goes by. New pieces of equipment will need to be mastered, with much learning implied. New situations will create new learning demands. Our own planned progression in our occupations will compete with unplanned events, both leading to the development of further knowledge, understanding, skills and attitudes.

(c) Lastly, *we ourselves* change; not just through the ageing process, although that is real enough, but experience will mould us so that we develop new perceptions and new interests. As we grow (not just an uncontrolled and uncontrollable process but often purposefully), we become individualised, "a hand-knitted human being" (Cohen and Leicester 2000: 72). This will create learning challenges.

It is important that we do not see these as separate categories, for human beings vary in their capacity to compartmentalise their lives. The comment that "a job is never merely a job" (Nowlen 1988: 69 in Walker 2001: 631) may be something of an overstatement, but many people find their occupation much more than simply a job; it is their personal interest. And it brings with it many social roles. Nevertheless, this threefold approach to experiential change over time may be a useful way of viewing the challenges and opportunities which bring about natural learning through life.

Faced with a changing person in a changing context, learning becomes a mixture of being responsive and being proactive. At times, we need to cope with new situations which are thrust upon us. At other times, we begin the process as something grabs our interest. If the learning is embedded in the process of living, it follows that most learning is located within some other activity: often a task we find ourselves facing. Much writing on adult learning has concentrated on the non-routine experiences of life, those events which throw us off balance and which bring about a disequilibrium and which therefore (it is argued) promote learning (Brookfield 2000: 88–101; Jarvis 1987: 79–80; Argyris and Schon 1974, 1978; Marsick and Watkins 1990: 15–24; Bourgeois 2000: 163). But routine events also bring with them learning. "We learn by walking" (Visser 2001: 467). Through learning, people "acquire their beliefs, knowledge and understandings [and I would add skills] that they need, beyond the ones they already have, in all the highways and byways of the... world" (Aspin and Chapman 2001: 20).

Learning, then, is all pervasive and it is active, not passive (Engstrom et al. 1999). It is not simply a matter of responding to stimuli, although stimuli will clearly play a part in encouraging learning. Nor is it simply a matter of 'receiving' other people's knowledge and skills which are 'imparted' to us, as so much of the literature on education suggests. We make the changes for ourselves, even when we are unconscious of doing so.

Again, learning is individual. Each of us learns for ourselves; someone else cannot 'learn' us. Even in social learning theories, ultimately "learning is a personal and natural process" (Smith 1982: 35). We may learn with, from and in association with others, but in the end all learning changes are made uniquely and individually and it is normally voluntary – we make learning changes because for some reason or other we have decided to do so (conditioning does play some part in learning but not much).

Finally, learning may be intentional and unintentional (Visser 2001: 454; Lucas 1983: 3). Life is full of learning events; incidental, even accidental, as well as purposeful. We can draw a distinction between learning events and learning practices. Learning events consist of those individual occasions of learning which occur from time to time. Learning practices consist of those cultured and structured ways of learning which each of us develops for ourselves. For among the many individual learning events, there are some activities which we engage in which are more intentional. Elsewhere, I have drawn attention to what I have called 'learning episodes', those occasions during our life's journey when we deliberately set out to learn something specific (Rogers 2002: 120–5). They may be social necessities or they may be the pursuit of personal interests. These are purposeful, structured occasions. We may not always be conscious that we are learning, for our consciousness may be directed towards a task we feel we need to accomplish, a problem we need to solve for ourselves, a satisfaction we need to attain. However, such occasions exist; and I suggest that we need to explore how each of the participants in our learning programmes engages with these natural events if we are to understand their own form of learning and to develop effective learning programmes for adults.

Learning involves a learner and his/her context. Merriam and Caffarella, in their masterly survey of the whole field of adult learning (Merriam and Caffarella 1999: 295, 399–403) suggest that learning consists of the interaction between learner, context and process. I have suggested elsewhere that there is a fourth element in this interaction, the kind of learning task, the content of learning (see Rogers 2002: 87–88). Others have suggested much the same: learning "cannot be pinned down to the head of the individual [learner] or to assigned tasks or to external tools or the environment but lies instead in the relations among them" (Lave 1988 cited in Cairns 2001: 20). Integrated learning is one key theme of today: Illeris (2002a), for example, has suggested that learning comprises three integrated dimensions: the cognitive, the affective and the social. It is this fact – that learning involves a complicated interaction between a number of elements – which accounts for the number of different schools of learning theories such as the behaviourist, the cognitive, the humanist, the social learning theories etc., each of them stressing one or at most two of these different components. All are searching for a single comprehensive understanding of learning, and all are partial, for they have omitted key elements in the learning formula.

Two kinds of learning

The search for a single all-embracing theory of learning would seem to be a fool's paradise. It has, I suggest, led many people astray for many years. Rather, I would wish to support those who suggest that there two main ways in which we all learn.

Many educators have repeatedly emphasised the existence of two quite distinct approaches. The pedigree goes back as far as Dewey who drew a distinction between education as a process of living and education as a preparation for future living (Snook 2001: 155). Houle (1961) spoke of two distinct ways of learning, one of "which functions as an instrument...to facilitate the [learner] into the logic of the present system" and the other which is "the practice of freedom". Freire (1972: 56–7) similarly distinguished between 'banking education' (the learning that domesticates) and 'problem-posing education' (a quite different kind of learning that liberates). Carl Rogers (1974) suggested that "the only learning which significantly influences behaviour is self-discovered, self-appropriated learning...which has been personally appropriated and assimilated in experience", which he contrasted with 'information transfer'. Like most other writers, he wrote of one kind of learning (humanistic learning) in positive terms and of the other (schooling) in negative terms. Similar value judgments have been made in the debate about formal and non-formal education (see Rogers, forthcoming). Revans (1980) contrasted 'action learning' (learning *by* doing) with more formal approaches (learning *for* doing). Others have contrasted the transfer of information with constructivist approaches to learning (e.g. Rahman 1993; see below).

We need to be careful about two things here. One is confusing learning with education (but in each of these cases, two distinct kinds of learning are presupposed as well as two different approaches to education). The other is that we must be wary of seeing things only in terms of a dichotomy, for polarisation may not be the most helpful way to look at learning today. Nevertheless, there is today a wide interest in informal learning as distinct from formal (and non-formal) learning (cf. *Encyclopedia of Informal Education*). Although not new (Beard (1976) spoke of incidental learning), a contrast between different kinds of learning is increasingly being drawn, and the terminology used in the formulation of this contrast is revealing. Thus the OECD, when talking about lifelong learning, acknowledges at least two kinds of learning when it says that it is "mainly concerned with planned, purposeful, systematic, worthwhile *learning* – not just any or all learning" (cited in Field and Leicester 2000: xvii). For others, formalised learning is to be distinguished from "informal learning as might occur through watching television, doing a job with a more experienced fellow worker, or participating in the institutions of civil society" (Enslin *et al.* 2001: 62; see also Richardson and Wolfe 2001; Visser 2001: 464 who speaks of "modern and traditional systems of knowledge and learning", and provides many references on page 451; Hager 2001: 79–92 – informal learning; McGivney 1999; Coffield 2000 – formal and informal learning; Marsick and Watson 1990: 15–24 – informal learning with incidental learning as a sub-set, and formal learning; Bjornavold 2000: 204 – non-formal learning; Eraut 2000 – incidental or implicit learning and explicit learning, etc.). In my earlier works, I argued that the natural informal learning processes used in the 'learning episodes' were different from the more formalised learning processes used in formal education.

It is this which accounts for the increasing attention being paid by educationalists to the everyday practices of both children and adults as an essential background and context for learning, the pool in which we all swim. Cole and Scribner (1974) were early advocates of such an approach but others have followed (Rogoff and Lave 1984; Lave 1988); as Llorente and Coben suggest, citing Wertsch (1991) "all these viewpoints take into account ways of social and psychological functioning which explicitly differ from practices seen in formal educational environments" (Llorente and Coben 2003).

The identification of two (and in some cases more than two[2]) kinds of learning has been around for many years (see e.g. Lucas 1983 and works cited in his paper). It takes various forms – a distinction between two kinds of learning processes and a distinction between two kinds of knowledge. The difference between tacit and explicit knowledge is becoming increasingly recognised. It can be seen in Lewin's distinction (Lewin and Grabbe 1945, discussed in Argyris 1993) between 'actionable knowledge'; that is, practical

---

[2] Habermas suggested initially three; instrumental, communicative and emancipatory learning, but later reduced these to two (Habermas 1972).

knowledge which is implemented in the everyday world, and what he called 'applicable knowledge'; that is, what is felt to be 'relevant' knowledge (theory) but not necessarily usable knowledge. Polyani (1966) spoke of tacit knowledge (subjective, intimately bound up with individual experience, contextualised and unique) and explicit knowledge (more abstract, independent of the knower, decontextualised and generalised), referring as an example to the range of knowledge involved in riding a bicycle. "In these cases, one does not really know what one knows" (Kidd 2002: 111). Tacit knowledge and skills are on the whole acquired and developed by tacit learning: as Aspin and his colleagues put it (ungrammatically), in tacit learning "the acquisition of knowledge, skills, values and understanding [is] different to that which people's experience of education and schooling heretofore has made them familiar" (Aspin *et al.* 2001: xliii).

Language acquisition and learning

The clearest distinction I know of the two different kinds of learning is that drawn by those who study the development of language skills. They have identified two ways of learning a language, one of which they call 'acquisition' and the other 'learning'.

Krashen (1982) is one of the clearest exponents of this distinction and what follows is taken largely from that work supplemented by others such as Hatch (1978)[3]. However, because 'acquisition' is still a form of learning, I am calling the former 'acquisition learning' and the latter 'formalised learning'[4].

The contrast is drawn between the way children on the whole learn their first language; a natural, very active process of 'imaginative

---

[3] I am grateful to Professor Brian Street for drawing my attention to the work of Krashen.

[4] I do not like the word 'acquisition' for this kind of learning, for it smacks of a deficit model and it can be misunderstood to mean the simple acquisition of information, the transfer of knowledge, rather than the active engagement with new knowledge and the development of new skills. It has been said that "learning is much more an evolutionary sense-making experiential process of development than a process of simple acquisition" (Brown 1990), by which is meant that simply acquiring information is not learning. However, the term is useful to distinguish it from formalised learning and as long as we remember that acquisition learning is very active, fully engaging with new situations, it can be useful. A better term, however, is needed.

playfulness'[5], and the way in which children (and adults) learn a subsequent language[6] in formal settings. The contrast is between natural learning and formalised learning: these are "two distinct and
independent ways of developing competence" (Krashen 1982: 10).
We may take this model of initial language learning as our starting
point for an analysis of acquisition learning. Some have suggested that
learning our first language is done without effort: for example, "the first
language ... which every normal human brain acquires with seeming
effortlessness" (Cenoz and Genesee 2001). Polyani (1966) too speaks of
tacit knowledge being acquired effortlessly. But acquisition learning is
not really "effortless", "passive acculturation" (Bagnall 2001: 36), for it
is certainly very active learning. It employs play, exploration and experimentation, trial and error, copying and mimicking, practising and self-
evaluation. It is in the fullest sense experiential learning (see Hager
2001: 86–7). It is not always conscious learning but it is based on the
agency of the learner, for the initiative comes mainly from the learner,
although rewards may be sought by the learner in terms of pleasing significant others. The recognition of the learning achieved is almost
always 'post-hoc'. Vygotsky suggests we engage in "learning to speak
and then finding out what it means, of clumsily taking over the forms
and tools of culture and then learning how to use them appropriately."
Like others, Hatch (1978: 401–435) suggests that we learn to use
(language) first and then appreciate the structure later.

Acquisition learning

Acquisition learning is, however, not confined to language learning,
or to children. We all use it all the time. When entering any new
social situation (a new job or moving to a new location, etc.), most
of the learning we do is acquisition learning, that "traditional lifelong

---

[5] There are some parts of first language learning which may be learned through formalised learning.
[6] Krashen talks about learning a 'second' language through more formal approaches,
but many people in multilingual cultures learn a second and even a third language
also through acquisition learning rather than through formalised learning. The distinction is between learning any language formally and learning any language
through acquisition learning.

cultural learning, the silent learning that takes place in societies regardless of its inscription in texts" (Kirpal 1976 cited in Edwards 2000: 9). Parenting, house ownership and citizenship are all examples of social role learning using acquisition learning. "When we join a new organization as an adult employee, we learn how to act, what to say and what is expected…not by someone conveying it verbally but from working in the organization over a period of time" (Dixon 1999: 25–26). Thus we learn not only to talk the language/discourse of that body but also many other things, such as how to move through the buildings, how to relate to different persons in that organisation and outside, and how to access resources, all through acquisition learning. There may of course be a more formal process of 'induction' but most of the initial acculturation is by acquisition learning. Refugees, as one or two recent studies have shown (Hannah 2000: 263–275; Cohen 1998), and recent entrants into retirement homes use acquisition learning to locate themselves and make sense of their new experience[7]. There are many occasions when adults use acquisition rather than formalised learning, just as there are other occasions when a more formalised process of learning is employed.

Acquisition learning is always concrete, immediate and confined to a specific activity; it is not concerned with general principles (see Hager 2001: 80–81). We learn new bus routes when we move to a new environment, but only those routes which apply to us, not the whole transport system. We learn how to manage new equipment such as cameras or videoplayers – but again only our own instruments, not generalities about these instruments. Such immediate acquisition learning is concerned with short-term purposes and will be suspended when the immediate task is felt to be accomplished to the satisfaction of the learner. It is of course voluntary or within the compulsion of the task. It is task- or problem-centred. It uses whatever materials can be found at hand: "People strive to satisfy purposes that have meaning within their community, and in their activities, they use tools, symbols and models that are culturally developed and transmitted" (Scribner 1988: 1). It does not see "knowledge…as strictly

---

[7] The theory of learning advanced by Lave and Wenger of legitimate peripheral participation is one form of this acquisition learning, although that theory can also incorporate more formalised approaches also; see Lave and Wenger 1991.

divided into disciplines... or partitioned... into diverse subjects such as English and Mathematics and History and Geography and Science ...[but] much more like a shifting set of webs... with which we try to make sense of the reality we share, and make it amenable to our understanding and control" (Aspin and Chapman 2001: 18). It thus draws upon all aspects perceived *by the learner* as relevant to the task in hand. A great deal of it is peer learning. And the evaluation is intrinsic, done in large part by the learner in terms of 'does it work?', its utility to achieve the goal set by the learner. Where such evaluation involves others, they are chosen by the learner (for example, by asking of a selected other, "is that [process, pronunciation, draft etc.] right?"). The material is submitted by the learner in a form determined by the learner for approval and correction, and the criteria for the assessment is its acceptability *in that specific context and for that specific purpose.* Acquisition learning is highly contextualised. It uses critical reflection on experience (Schon 1983), transformation of meanings (Mezirow *et al.* 2001) and constructivist learning (Rorty 1979; Steffe and Gale 1995; Phillips 1995), but always within an immediate context and limited to that context.

Unconscious learning

Vygotsky (1996) and others have described this process as learning unconsciously and spontaneously in the course of accomplishing some self-set task of immediate relevance to our life[8]. This idea of unconscious (or implicit) learning is not of course new. Dewey as long ago as 1897 said that

> ... all education proceeds by the participation of the individual in the social consciousness of the race ... This process... is constantly shaping the individual's powers, saturating his [sic] habits, training his ideas and arousing his feelings and emotions. Through this unconscious education, the individual gradually comes to share in the intelligent and moral resources which humanity has succeeded in getting together.
>
> (Dewey 1971(v): 84)

Bateson (1973) (see Bron and Schemmann 2000: 27) suggested that proto-learning ("monitored, designed and planned" learning) was distinct from deutero-learning ("seldom... consciously controlled").

---

[8] Not all the tasks which form the subject of acquisition learning are self-set.

However, this distinction has in recent years come to assume greater prominence among writers on adult learning. As Krashen puts it, both the process and the learning outcomes of language acquisition are subconscious. Firstly, the learners are not usually aware of the fact that they are acquiring language but are only aware of the fact that they are using language for communication, and secondly, the result of language acquisition, the acquired competence, is also subconscious. Dixon speaks of

> ... another way of learning that ... occurs over time and without conscious awareness ... the way young children, for example, learn language, by hearing it and creating patterns in the words and syntax, yet remaining unaware of the patterns. The child is aware only that he or she is able to communicate, but not of the syntax learned to facilitate the construction of sentences. It is not only children who learn tacitly. Much of the knowledge we as adults carry about ourselves and others is learned through tacit comprehension ... from exposure to the culture in which we live.

(Dixon 1999: 25)

Others too have pointed this out: "A great deal of the acquisition of human culture occurs through this pre-conscious process of learning"; "the everyday learning from experience which usually passes unnoticed" (Jarvis 1987: 30; Usher 1993, cited in Hager 2001: 86). By partaking in social and vocational lifeworlds, we all learn knowledge and skills more or less unconsciously. Elsdon and his colleagues (1995), for example, point to the situated, unrecognised and often unconscious learning through working with voluntary organisations, and Foley too sees much learning within the 'new social movements' (Foley 1999). Engstrom (1994) contrasts "traditional book learning" with "the acquisition of fixed routines by practice and imitation ... There are two kinds of [learning]. One is the influence people experience in the context of other activities. This happens, for instance, through games and hobbies, the arts and entertainment, or in connection with political activities. When [learning] is subordinated in this way to some other activity, it is mainly a tacit experience." He contrasts this with guided learning.

Task-conscious learning

Some, then, have referred to this kind of learning as 'unconscious' or implicit learning. "Implicit learning is essentially learning without

awareness. Knowledge that has been acquired implicitly is knowledge that has been acquired and held largely without conscious effort." Thus we can speak of "implicit learning... in the absence of intention to learn... in the absence of awareness that one is learning, and in such a way that the resulting knowledge is difficult to express" (Reber 2003: 486; Cleeremans 2003: 491). Engstrom suggests that in his first category of education, "learning is often incidental and piecemeal: it may happen practically without conscious effort" (Engstrom 1987: 5). In the light of recent work on consciousness (Wilber 1982, 1983; Thomas 1994; Kegan 1982; Scott 1996; Simonsen 2000[9]), it may be better to speak of the consciousness as being of the task rather than of the learning. I would therefore wish to speak of this as *task-conscious learning*. The learner is not conscious of the fact that she/he is learning, but is conscious of the task in hand. At times, some increased awareness of the learning involved surfaces: for example, when a new incumbent in office speaks as being 'on a steep learning curve', by which they normally mean that, engaged as they are on the essential day-to-day tasks of that office, they are aware of how much they need to learn and how much learning they are achieving through the successful or unsuccessful completion of those tasks. However, in most cases it is "not recognised by the individual concerned as learning, and [it is] not manifest in some course or other purposeful educational activity" (Duke 2001: 508–9). It is learning *en passant* (Reischmann 1986: 3, cited in Jarvis 1987: 30). The primary focus in all of this is on immediate task achievement, not learning for some future activity. The learning, then, is limited to the task in hand.

Learning and memory

Here we need to draw upon contemporary memory theory. Some writers today, rather than speaking of short-term and long-term memory, have taken to using the terms 'working memory' and 'storage memory' (Dixon 1999; Mulligan 2003; Bjorklund et al. 2003). While there is something mechanical about such constructs, influenced as they often are by artificial intelligence and computer

---

[9] This is different from the (class) consciousness of organic intellectuals of Gramsci; but it does relate to his self–other consciousness and the concept of alienation (Cohen 1998).

ideologies, nevertheless the change in formulation can be helpful. Working memory is based on the *use* of the material so that learning, storing and especially recall come about through the performance of some task, not through deliberate storage of knowledge. Thus in the course of a task, existing knowledge, skills and beliefs are drawn upon and used without consciousness of drawing on memory. This refers to what is often called tacit knowledge, tacit comprehension and tacit skills which acquisition learning is constantly laying down and revising (Polyani 1966; Reingold and Ray 2003). Acquisition learning relies more on the storage memory than on the working memory which more formalised learning tends to use. For formalised learning seeks to locate new knowledge, including rules, and skills in the working memory: we know that we know this or that we can do that. Formalised learning, however, may on occasion also lay down knowledge and some skills in the storage memory, in which case it relies on the creation of various conscious cues, structures and strategies to recall such tacit knowledge and skills when needed for a task.

Formalised learning

Formalised learning is very different from acquisition learning. As the learning of a language through formal instruction indicates (Krashen 1982), it is more concerned with general principles, with commonly accepted rules (grammar etc.) – it is decontextualised, applicable across a number of different contexts, and the learning processes also differ.

Facilitated learning

Formalised learning arises from the process of facilitating learning. We need to be careful in making that definition, for some elements of facilitation comes into most forms of acquisition learning which (as we have seen) includes imitation and play as well as exploration and discovery learning. But formalised learning is learning which has been constructed by others for the purpose of consciously assisting learning. Formalised learning is based on some form of 'teaching' in its widest possible sense.

Teaching today is being re-examined. At times, this reassessment is expressed in radical terms. "The…impossibility of teaching" (Felman 1982: 21) has been noted. "Knowledge cannot be transferred…learning is always an act of self-search and discovery. In this search and discovery, one may be stimulated and assisted, but cannot be taught" (Rahman 1993: 219, 222). The role of the teacher is simply "planning the conditions of the learning environment" (Visser 2001: 456). But more frequently it is now recognised that this reassessment is leading to a reassertion of "what good teachers have been doing for centuries – putting the focus on facilitating the goals of learning" (Aspin et al. 2001: xliii), stimulating and assisting the learner in learning.

However, facilitating learning is to formalise it, to structure it, to break it down into manageable and sequential elements. Formalised learning is 'educative learning', to be distinguished from "the simple accumulation of experience" (Bagnall 1990, cited in Aspin and Chapman 2001: 13). Formalised learning is largely under the control of the guide. It is planned, compartmentalised and set out in a curriculum for ease of mastery. It is often content-oriented rather than process- or problem-oriented. There is a component of dependency involved in formalised learning. The material is simplified, sequenced, systematised and seen by the guide as complete (Krashen 1982: 58–9). It is based on "indirect experience and the use of representational systems" (Chapman and Aspin 2001: 423) rather than or as well as on direct experience. It has externally set outcomes and standards. It uses special materials prepared and/or chosen by the facilitator. Rules are learned first and then practised later. It is largely or wholly "uncontextualised – i.e. there is an emphasis on general principles rather than their specific applications" (Hager 2001: 81). It is universal rather than contextualised (Duke 2001: 518). Its material is often more abstract than acquisition learning, generalised, decontextualised, and intended for long-term and widespread application.

Formalised learning usually uses working memory. It stores knowledge and skills which we consciously know we possess and can use. It does also store some knowledge and skills into the storage memory, and it is therefore concerned with developing strategies for accessing and recalling stored knowledge and skills from this long-term memory. It relies on conscious memorisation rather than on memorisation by use, developing strategies such as mnemonics, rote learning of mathematical tables or lists of words, spellings and vocabularies, etc.

Formalised learning is specifically planned to achieve a socially determined and desirable purpose (Peters 1966) and therefore its evaluation is extrinsic – its achievements will be assessed and evaluated in terms of that purpose. This is most clearly expressed today in many of the publications on lifelong learning/education which see it as important to the economic and social life of the nation (cf. for example, Henry *et al.* 2001). For although formalised learning claims to be concerned with universals, with general rules, it is nevertheless still a sociocultural construct created within a specific context. Although through globalisation one form of it has become common to most educational programmes throughout the world, this remains what it was in origin; a Western construct exported to other cultures. There is no God-given formalisation of learning, simply frequently-agreed ways of breaking up learning matter and assisting the process of the development of explicit knowledge and skills.

Because of its inherent nature to facilitate certain chosen and desirable learning goals, formalised learning advocates working with groups of "people of like minds, at about similar kinds of cognitive development, and capable of similar rates of progress – but not necessarily of similar chronological ages – forming a self-conscious critical mass" (Aspin and Chapman 2001: 22). Although formalised learning sometimes goes beyond this (especially in open and distance learning or self-directed learning projects (Tough 1979)), it is the process of facilitating learning which has led to the development of formal programmes and systems of education, the establishment of 'classes' and other forms of learning groups.

Sites of learning

Formalised learning is not, however, confined to formal settings such as school classrooms or college lecture halls. It is much wider than this, extending to training courses and the informal use of training manuals and other forms of publication, to non-formal education, and to open- and distance-learning programmes. It is therefore "more than the formal school system. It includes equally the various alternative pathways to learning *whose basic underlying assumptions – as expressed in acquisition/delivery metaphors and the treatment of knowledge as a commodity – are the same ones that underlie the formal school system*" (Visser 2001: 459, my italics). Formalised learning is more than schooling, for it includes all forms of assisted learning.

We thus need to distinguish between the sites of learning and the processes of learning. Resnick (1987) tends to equate the two, suggesting that the learning that goes on inside formal settings (schools and colleges but including situations involving the use of textbooks, distance learning sites, workplace/on-the-job training, etc.) is different in quality from what she calls 'out-of-school learning' (in what are often called 'non-formal settings'). Using the same kinds of distinction as Carl Rogers indicated, she suggested that the former tends to be individualised, competitive, mainly mental, decontextualised, generalised and generalisable learning, and that this can be contrasted with 'out-of-school' learning which uses tools rather than minds alone, is collaborative, contextualised and situation-specific. Now, I suggest that it is true that two kinds of sites of learning can be identified: formal settings and informal settings. Equally, it is true that at least two different sets of learning processes, acquisition and formalised learning, can be seen. But the two kinds of learning are not always and firmly to be equated with the two kinds of sites of learning, as Resnick suggests. There is a matrix which can be seen here.

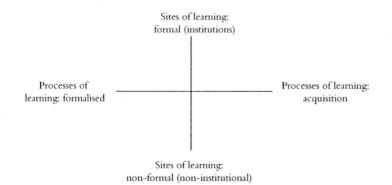

Sites of learning:
formal (institutions)

Processes of learning: formalised   Processes of learning: acquisition

Sites of learning:
non-formal (non-institutional)

Both acquisition learning and formalised learning take place in both formal and informal settings.

I do not wish to be too prescriptive about this, for the range of different sites of learning is wide and the range of different processes of learning is equally large, and therefore the mix of these will be great. However, it may be suggested that when many adults go into formal sites of learning, they tend to adopt formalised approaches to learning which they associate from experience with those sites; much formal education encourages this. What is more, those who have been most exposed to formal education may also tend to use formalised learning even in non-formal settings (in the home, in the workplace, in social settings, etc.), for they feel more comfortable with these processes once they have identified that what they are doing is learning[10]. This may help to account for the fact that most of those who participate in adult education programmes are persons who already have a good deal of experience in formal education. However, acquisition learning processes continue to be used in formal settings, just as on occasion formalised learning processes are used in informal settings. Perhaps we need to learn that when adults engage in their own purposeful learning, they choose those sites of learning available to them which they feel are most appropriate to their situations as well as to their preferred learning processes, and that they choose those processes which they are most comfortable with.

Conscious learning

The key seems to be the consciousness of learning. Formalised learning is used when the learner is conscious that the task they are engaged in is that of learning. Formalised learning is conscious learning. As Vygotsky suggests, when talking about what he calls the 'zone of proximal development' (that context of learning which lies "under...the guidance or in collaboration with more capable peers"), "by using the help of others, he [sic – the learner] gains consciousness and perspective under his own control, reaches 'higher ground'" (Bruner 1983: 140, cited in Cairns 2001: 21; see Wertsch 1985). The task then of the facilitator of learning is to help make conscious the subconscious or task-conscious learning of the acquisition process. Freire (1972: 20–44) spoke of the kind of learning

---

[10] See Shirley Brice Heath's work 1983 cited below (page 37).

based on the development of critical consciousness "in which men [sic], not as recipients but as knowing subjects, achieve a deepening awareness both of the sociocultural reality which shapes their lives and of their capacity to transform that reality." Today there is some scepticism about those programmes which talk about the ideas of 'learning to learn' (Dewey 1916: 53): some now speak of "the false premise ... that there is such a thing as a generic skill of learning how to learn ... that can meaningfully be taught to people" (Barrow and Keeney 2001: 56). Nevertheless, formalised learning is posited on a consciousness of learning goals and strategies, of ways of breaking material down so that it can be mastered; and the evaluation is based on how much has been learned.

I would therefore wish to call this kind of learning *learning-conscious learning* as distinct from *task-conscious learning*. Learning itself is the task (see Ryle 1949, cited in Aspin *et al.* 2001: 11). What formalised learning does is to make learning more conscious in order to enhance it. Just as with breathing, which we do mostly unconsciously but which from time to time we may become conscious of so as to enhance it (for athletics or singing or medical reasons etc), so too learning which we all do unconsciously can from time to time become more conscious so that it can be enhanced: "putting a focus on facilitating the goal of learning how to learn, including instilling a love for learning [i.e. more formalised learning] and command over it" (Aspin *et al.* 2001: xliii). Both adults and children are capable of metacognition, of knowing on some occasions that they are learning and what kinds of strategies they are using in learning-conscious learning (Smith and Pourchot 1998).

The advantages and disadvantages of both kinds of learning

There are then two different kinds of learning – the natural process others have called acquisition or unconscious learning, but which I would wish to call *task-conscious learning* which goes on throughout life whenever we engage in new cultural settings or need to cope with our everyday experiences; and formalised or conscious learning (what I have called *learning-conscious learning*), guided episodes of learning (for a contemporary contrast between formalised learning in a wide range of settings and informal (subconscious) learning, see Hager 2001: 80–81).

These two kinds of learning are not confined to specific contexts of learning or programmes of learning. Indeed, one of the most important consequences of this realisation is the appreciation that acquisition learning continues even when the learner is engaged in formalised learning. In the classroom, which may be regarded as a sociocultural centre in much the same way as banks, churches and supermarkets are sociocultural centres, spaces where specific cultured practices take place (see Bloome *et al.* 1989), students are learning a great deal through acquisition as well as formalised learning. Much of the so-called hidden curriculum is being learned from the teacher and from the setting through acquisition learning. Much is being learned from peer students and from persons other than the teacher who from time to time engage with the students. Cook and Yanow (1993) seem to refer to this distinction when they talk of "the learning and social-ization" that goes on at school (socialisation is of course learning). Equally this is true of "work-place learning... [which includes] the formal on-the-job training as well as the informal learning that occurs *as people perform their work*" (Hager 2001: 80, my emphasis). What we have then is not two different kinds of education in different locations but two different ways of learning which go on within the same contexts.

Acquisition learning, like formalised learning, is almost always assisted in some way or other, for it takes place within a social con-text. The active learner usually chooses the peer facilitator and 'bounces off' ideas and practices for feedback. Such interaction may or may not include elements of formalised learning with it, and the decision as to how much of such formalisation of learning should be included can at times be an issue with the peer facilitator. To give an example: In the course of commenting on a draft paper in a work situation, an instance arose recently relating to a description of a meeting due to be held. The phrase 'manager's conference' had been written instead of 'managers' conference'; in this context, the mean-ing was incorrect and it needed to be changed. The task in hand however was not a learning task (the paper was not submitted to a teacher for English grammar) but a check-before-circulation task. Thus the question in dealing with this was whether to promote usable learning about the issue involved or not. Amendment of the text without further comment would leave it to the author herself to try to draw the general conclusion through acquisition learning and to apply this in future; but the author might simply accept the correction without understanding the reasons for the change. A more detailed course would be to explain the different meanings of the two phrases ('the conference for which the manager (singular) was responsible' or 'the conference which all the managers (plural) needed to attend'); this would help to an understanding of the necessity for the change in this situation, but again the writer would be left to deduce the general rule for future texts. But a more detailed explanation of the apostrophe and its application to singular and plural nouns which would have led to the avoidance of this problem of meaning in future, might have alienated the writer and interrupted the flow of the interaction. The decision depended on the relationship between the peer facilitator and the 'learner' and the assumptions made about the existing comprehension of the latter.

The same is true of all task-related learning situations, whether within acquisition or formalised learning situations. In hands-on music, art or history, for example, or in the experiential learning of computer skills, management and languages, the balance between the practical case study work and the creation of frames of reference for understanding is a matter of balance which lies with the facilitator of the learning. The issue is how far the person engaged in helping forward the learning can assume that the learner is capable of drawing their own general principles and how far the interactive process can be advanced or hindered by making the general principles explicit; how far understanding is left to the learner to develop from the concrete tasks of the learning process or how far it is set out explicitly. All who facilitate the learning of others make assumptions about the 'other(s)' on which they base the approach to learning they adopt and the actions that flow from that approach.

Both forms of learning have their own value. Unfortunately, there has been a tendency in the past to glorify one or other approach to learning while demeaning the other kind of learning. Thus, on the one hand, those who assert the significance of informal learning often point to the disadvantages of formal education, seen as schooling. The setting of prescribed outcomes to the learning process is often condemned as being dehumanising (Freire 1972). On the other hand, those who value formal learning, wherever it is sited, tend to ignore or demean acquisition learning as unimportant. Thus, those who (as we have seen) continue to assert that there are some persons who have "done no learning since leaving school" are clearly excluding all the subconscious or unconscious task-conscious learning from this statement. For them, such acquisition learning does not count. This is not only unfortunate: it is actually denying the value of such learning. Acquisition learning, the process of acculturation which we all use when engaged in task performance, is very important, and the processes employed in it are of particular significance for those who seek to help adults to learn.

The importance of acquisition learning

A number of examples of the significance of such informal learning may be given.

Tacit learning and mechanical learning

First, it is through acquisition learning that we all develop much of the tacit knowledge and tacit comprehension that we use when completing tasks or fulfilling purposes (Sallis and Jones 2002; Schon 1983). Unconsciously, when engaged in tasks through which we learn, we lay down "the beliefs, knowledge and understanding" that we have already seen we need in order to perform in life (see Aspin and Chapman 2001: 20 cited above). We do not know that we know them, yet we call upon them when engaged in the performance of any task.

To call such learning 'mechanical learning' as against 'meaningful learning' is a mistake. What is sometimes called mechanical learning is often the process of using tacit knowledge and skills for the completion of some task without being aware that one is using such knowledge or skills. A farmer planting plants at certain intervals, a craftsman engaging in some craft activity 'mechanically', a parent reacting mechanically to certain issues as they arise are all calling upon tacit knowledge and skills developed through previous experience. The 'mechanical' use of calculations which we all engage in from time to time (on the buses or trains; in shops etc.) is actually meaningful activity in those contexts using tacit knowledge and skills which have been laid down mainly through acquisition learning. I say 'mainly', for we need to be wary at this point. A simple equivalence of tacit knowledge and comprehension with acquisition learning is not possible. Some of our tacit knowledge and comprehension is developed through formalised learning. We learn (for example) numerical tables formally by rote until they have passed into our subconscious, so that we know as it were by instinct that the product of six sevens is 42. We may have more difficulty with deciding whether the product of six nines is 54 or 56, in which case we may call upon certain cues we have learned, again formally (e.g. that each of the products of the 'nine times' table always add up to nine, so that six nines must be 54, the two digits of which add up to nine, rather than 56). One objective of formalised learning is to lay down some elements of tacit knowledge and comprehension as well as more conscious learning and to provide cues and structures to access that tacit knowledge.

However, most of our tacit knowledge comes from task-conscious learning, from the acquisition through experience and through the processes of play, exploration and role imitation which form the active ingredients of acquisition learning of new insights and knowledge. The natural learning which all persons do, both young persons and adults, throughout their lives cannot be dismissed as insignificant.

The development of learning styles

Secondly, it is through such subconscious acquisition learning that we each develop for ourselves the various individually preferred learning styles which Kolb and others have demonstrated (Kolb 1976; Honey and Mumford 1986). It is not through the formalised learning that individuals come to be activists or reflectors, to be theorists or experimenters; rather, it is through the unconscious learning which goes on in all situations, the acculturation, the task-conscious learning which lays down for each of us the processes with which we find ourselves most comfortable.

The development of barriers to formalised learning

Thirdly, and perhaps most importantly for those engaged in the provision of lifelong learning opportunities, task-conscious learning may create barriers to the learning we wish to promote. One of the most important of these is the self-horizon (see below, page 55) which we all develop for ourselves, the limits which we impose on ourselves (the "I'm no good at maths" syndrome). This is part of the process of acquisition learning. Similarly, the existing knowledge of the learners can on occasion prevent the acceptance of new knowledge, and this becomes even more potent a barrier if the individual does not know that they know it. Part of the process of making subconscious learning more conscious in formalised learning is to bring such knowledge from the background storage memory into the more conscious foreground working memory.

The interaction of acquisition learning and formalised learning

There are other ways in which acquisition learning lays down the foundations on which formalised learning is built; just as formalised learning will interact with and affect acquisition learning. "For those of us whose main activity is teaching... it could be... important to understand how learning in the informal sector interacts with formal teaching" (Lucas 1983: 3). The most important of these is the relationship between theory and practice.

Relating theory and practice

The concern of acquisition task-conscious learning with the immediate and the concrete has led to its identification with practical knowledge rather than theoretical knowledge. Although there is today some wish to "de-emphasise the spurious theory-and-practice" distinction (Yates and Chandler 1991: 133–4), nevertheless it is still true that acquisition learning is concerned with the practical, the concrete, rather than the universal, the abstract; it is situated learning, the application of knowledge and skills in real situations for real purposes. And the relative value of each kind of learning has often been debated. The work of Aristotle has been cited several times in this respect:

> ... practical wisdom is not concerned with universals only – it [wisdom] must also recognize the particulars. For it is practical, and practice is concerned with particulars. This is why some who are not knowledgeable, and especially those who have experience, are more practical than those who are knowledgeable.
>
> (Aristotle; cf. citations in Jarvis 2000: 53;
> Field and Leicester 2000: 53)

It is sometimes argued that such acquisition learning (in language or in other spheres), because it is unconscious of learning, does not result in the development of universal or general rules ('theories' in the theorem sense rather than the hypothesis sense). Thus, for example, it has been suggested that in language acquisition we are generally not aware of the syntax of the language we have acquired. Instead, we have a 'feel' for correctness, and "errors feel wrong, even if we do not consciously know what rule was violated" (Krashen 1982: 10). More widely, Schon talks of 'knowing-in-action' as being tacit knowledge in that the practitioner uses this knowledge but cannot express it, and Polyani refers to 'personal knowledge' in which the user follows rules that are "not known as such to the performer" (cited in Hager 2001: 82–3).

But this would seem not always to be true. In much informal language learning, some form of (often unconscious) rules or general principles do appear to be created or absorbed by the learners. Indeed, the development of expertise, alleged to be one of the key differences between the adult and the child (Hager 2001: 87–88), seems to consist in the ability to draw general rules from the specific learning activities of the unconscious acquisition learning. This can be seen, for example, in those so-called 'good mistakes' in which a language learner will apply a general principle even to situations when it does not actually apply – for instance, putting a plural 's' onto words which do not take them, like 'children' or 'sheep' etc. Gee has pointed out in his study of the learning of computer games that general principles can be formed through acquisition learning and applied to different situations more or less unconsciously (Gee 2003). Nevertheless, these rules appear to be held subconsciously, rarely if ever brought through into consciousness. It is one of the values of learning-conscious learning that such rules become available to the consciousness for application in different contexts.

The value of formalised learning

The value of formalised learning has not always been recognised. It has often come under attack from non-formal educators and deschoolers such as Illich and radicals like Freire. For example, "the traditional educational model where instructors impart knowledge to passive students has been repeatedly challenged, and newer models indicate that effective learning is an active process of discovery by the individual, with the teacher, if present at all, acting as a guide" (Hanna and Haillet 2001: 691). Even some establishment figures have seen formalised learning in largely negative terms: thus Faure and others were suggesting in 1972 that what they called 'the academic model' was out of date and obsolete (Faure *et al.* 1972), and Dore (1976) spoke of schooling as being 'anti-educational'. Rahman spoke in disparaging terms about the 'transfer of information' approach to learning (see above).

Others have recognised that for tacit knowledge to be shared, it needs to be formalised and articulated (Wertsch 1985; Scribner *et al.* 1991). "One of the difficulties in sharing tacit knowledge is the need for formalization" (Kidd 2002: 111). The sharing of knowledge (for example in the workplace or between generations) necessitates the development of conscious strategies of mastering a field of study. The internalisation of general rules which make knowledge and skills applicable in other arenas; "the ability to see the whole as well as the detail; the disposition not to feel trapped in a false dilemma of 'either-or' choices between different levels of the same reality" (Visser 2001: 450) are some of the benefits which formalised learning brings to acquisition learning. It is above all the facts that learning becomes conscious, that through formalised learning the building up of larger and more complex structures becomes possible, that universals can be identified, recognised, recalled and applied to other practical contexts, and that the evaluation is based on the learning of such generalities and their application, that the greatest value of formalised learning can be seen. Universals (and an understanding of their limitations) form the foundation for critical analysis of any situation.

The limitations of acquisition learning

All this needs to be set against some of the limitations of acquisition learning. First, for example, tacit knowledge is limited "in that though practitioners know it, they cannot express it" (Schon 1983, cited in Hager 2001: 83). Because they do not know that they have the knowledge, because it is unconscious knowledge, the generalisability of what is learned is not recognised. It remains usable only in specific contexts where it is applied as unconsciously as it was learned (tacit comprehension). Formalised learning is needed both to help with the development of techniques to increase the knowledge held in the storage memory and to access this knowledge more purposefully through the conscious use of structures, cues and rules.

Secondly, acquisition is less likely to lead to critical reflection on experience than formalised learning, for acquisition learning is "strongly characterized" by instrumentalism "and contextualization of learning [both of which] are strongly counter-critical" (Bagnall 2001: 44). It is true that both forms of learning are frequently subverted to prevent critical reflection; but acquisition or task-conscious learning, drawing as it does on the accepted norms of the immediate sociocultural context and seeking its evaluation in terms of what works, of what proves to be acceptable to the chosen evaluator, will tend to be normative. Language acquisition is clearly an example of task-conscious learning being prescriptive, the form of language learned being that acceptable within the immediate context with its own accents and intonations rather being in a more widely acceptable form. Although there will be a measure of reflection within acquisition learning ("things do not need to be like this; they can be different"), on the whole acquisition learning will tend to assist conformity rather than individuation.

There is a third major limitation of acquisition or task-conscious learning. Real-life tasks may not be the best arena for learning and experimentation; the 'real' consequences could be serious. To learn how to cook through cooking a real meal for an important guest is to invite disaster. It is true that in many contexts, the only way to learn is through acquisition learning in real contexts (parenting, for example). But in general real life does not make for a viable context for learning innovations. That is a role which formalised, facilitated, learning-conscious learning can fill.

Combining both kinds of learning

There is today a tendency in many countries towards using more formalised forms of learning. As we have seen, much of the discourse of lifelong learning is directed towards opening up more formalised learning inside educational campuses, or towards the creation of more formalised learning programmes in life-related sites such as the workplace (Aspin *et al.* 2002; Istance *et al.* 2002). Again, trends such as the Literacy Hour in UK schools are coming to rely more on formalised learning than trying to use what is sometimes called home-based learning or acquisition task-conscious learning: thus the six-year old who comes home saying that she has been learning about ordinal numbers at school today!

Calls for bringing together both forms of learning, however, remain persistent. Krashen, for example, calls upon language teachers to bring more acquisition "life-based" learning into their formalised learning, contextualising the universals: "if acquisition is central and [formalised] learning more peripheral [to the life experience of all learners], then the goal of our pedagogy should be to encourage acquisition" (Krashen 1982: 20, 58–59). Rather than ignoring or demeaning acquisition learning, it is urged that it is both possible and desirable to build on this process, to take task-conscious learning into learning-conscious learning by exploring any real learning situation in terms of the processes involved, and yet at the same time to go beyond acquisition learning. It has even been suggested that formalised learning programmes without acquisition learning can be counter-effective: "an environment in which learning is largely limited to the one-dimensional single-mode processes that characterize most of the traditional formal schooling context is antithetical to true learning" (Visser 2001: 456). As Visser says, the formal model of learn first and then act needs to be replaced with a combined model of act and learn together: learn by acting (see also Engstrom's theory of activity, Engstrom *et al.* 1999). It is possible to "redefine … educational systems so that they place greater emphasis on less-formal approaches" (Aspin *et al.* 2001: xxxvii), to concretise formalised learning, bringing into it task-conscious learning: "a higher education professional preparation course that lacks such experiential learning is inherently flawed" (Hager 2001: 87). It should also be an objective of learning facilitators to bring some more formalised learning into the acquisition processes. To engage in task-conscious learning through specific activities (tasks) alone without making conscious the conclusions which such exercises demonstrate is to render these activities (despite all the acquisition learning accomplished) less than fully effective.

Both aspects of this interchange are of course already being undertaken in different circumstances. There seem to be times in our own learning episodes when we combine elements of both. Formalisation for example takes place in several contexts of acquisition learning: formal induction programmes, for example, run by offices and factories. Shirley Brice Heath shows how many middle-class formally-educated parents introduce elements of formalised learning even into initial language learning (Heath 1983). Equally, some elements of task-conscious learning are being introduced into formalised learning (Bernstein 1975, 1996) and it is increasingly being recognised that both kinds of learning need to be drawn upon:

> We envisage a dual approach to education and training... On the one hand, there should be a range of context-specific courses offered to meet the needs prioritised by the [learners]... On the other hand, there should be an initiative to ensure access to more formal decontextualised education.
>
> (Breier et al. 1996: 232)

Demand-led and supply-led learning programmes need to go hand-in-hand.

> There is... a need to overcome the shortcomings of the disciplinary structure of knowledge, moving beyond multidisciplinarity and interdisciplinarity, to start seeing things in a transdisciplinary perspective. In short, we need to rediscover the unity of knowledge; we need to rediscover the relationship between action and learning.
>
> (Visser 2001: 461; Morin, cited in Visser 2001: 468n5)

"Educational provision and engagement [need] to be contextualized, to be optimally embedded in the adaptive life tasks to which the learning is directed" (Bagnall 2001: 39, citing Gustavsson 1997, Kozlowski 1995). Nonaka and Takeuchi call for the creation of new knowledge through the dialogic interaction between tacit knowledge and explicit knowledge (Nonaka and Takeuchi 1995; for a useful summary, see Kidd 2002: 113–4). 'Play with the risks removed' is a useful way in which to describe such a process of bringing acquisition learning into formalised learning – certainly a more comfortable context for learning skills such as computer processing than 'learning through doing for real'. The ICT revolution has helped in this: "Nowadays, learning through multi-media technology is not like that found in the more traditional school setting: in these days, learning, acquiring knowledge and probing understanding...can be regarded as play" (Aspin and Chapman 2001: 10).

But it is conscious play: this mixture is Vygotsky's making conscious the subconscious learning of acquisition learning. The most effective learning programmes are those in which the learners "become conscious of their implicit theories about learning...of their own thinking and learning strategies...learners gain conscious awareness of un- or sub-conscious learning through strategies such as reflection, intuition, imagination and fantasy" (Griffey and Kelleher 1996: 3–9, cited in Chapman and Aspin 2001: 423).

This is not a cobbling together of two incompatibles, bringing elements such as peer learning (Boud *et al.* 2001) from acquisition learning into formalised learning. Rather there is interaction between the two kinds of learning. For example, formalised learning will encourage the rote learning of numerical tables until they become unconscious tools, put away in storage memory, tacit knowledge. Thus not only will subconscious learning be made more conscious, but some conscious learning will become subconscious. There are considerable congruities between the two kinds of learning (Llorente and Coben 2003).

The key distinction seems to be that whereas formalised learning today on the whole ignores the specific learning needs and the experiences which each of the student participants brings to the learning situation, using *only* the generalised prepared material, the integration of acquisition learning with formalised learning will utilise the personal experience and inputs which each of the learners brings into the formalised learning programme. Such a programme will work to meet the individual as well as general learning needs of each learner. Exactly how this integration can be done must depend on the teacher, the subject, the context and the particular group of learners. It is not easy, especially within the larger teaching groups which lifelong learning education is creating today. However, trying to understand the home-based, task-conscious or acquisition learning of the learners is an essential characteristic of all teachers in any formalised learning situation (Engstrom 1987).

Examples

A number of examples will help to demonstrate this argument. I watch my daughter-in-law with one of my grandchildren learning to cook. He takes the initiative: "What are you doing, Mummy?" She seizes the moment. He drags up a stool in the kitchen. She gives him tasks to do. He seeks evaluation: "Is that right, Mummy?". A mixture of acquisition and formalised learning is going on with the introduction into the cooking process of a number of essentially unnecessary activities designed to help him to learn something. Constant decisions are being made as to whether to stop every now and again to make conscious what he is learning or leave him to develop such consciousness for himself. Mentorships and other forms of work-based learning ('sitting with Nellie' as it has been called) are clear examples of cases where acquisition learning (the performance of real tasks evaluated by task-performance) and formalised learning (the performance of artificial tasks designed to promote and evaluate significant 'bytes' of learning) combine in different ways and to different degrees. In apprenticeships, watching the 'master' [sic], imitating, practising, and experimenting (within limits) all occur, as well as set pieces of instruction and predetermined and sequenced activities intended to bring about the mastery of particular elements of the production process make up the total programme (on apprenticeships, see Lave and Wenger 1991; Merriam and Caffarella 1999: 243–5; Steedman *et al.* 1998; Guile and Young 2001). The assessment/ accreditation of prior experiential learning (APEL) is an example where some socially approved forms of acquisition learning are formally recognised (Evans 1987, 1992).

Literacy and numeracy learning

Perhaps a rather more detailed case study can indicate ways in which acquisition learning and formalised learning need each other. The development of literacy and numeracy skills are a matter of considerable concern in most countries today. But most literacy and numeracy learning programmes, both for adults and children, tend to ignore the acquisition learning that has already taken place and which continues to take place during the learning programme. All adults, literate or non-literate, will have learned a good deal about literacy through acquisition learning. Through the tasks which they have faced, through watching others who face or engage with such tasks, even those in non-literate contexts have developed tacit beliefs, knowledge and attitudes towards literacy and towards themselves in relation to literacy (Cole and Scribner 1974). Many children learn to read and write through task-conscious learning rather than formalised learning; but they will need formalised learning to make this informal learning more consistent and usable in different contexts. Equally, recent research in several different contexts has revealed that a significant number of adults have acquired informal literacies (reading the Bible and hymn books, for example, or keeping notes for themselves of their own accounts) through acquisition learning without going to primary school or adult literacy classes – they have learned from real life, including others who may have been to formal school or adult class. But when they come to adult literacy learning programmes, they learn (by acquisition learning) that such literacies are not important; these are ignored by their teachers and they do not form part of the learning programme or learning materials. This will imply attitudes of the teachers and educational planners to the learners as well as to the learning. It is surely necessary, if we are to be effective in adult literacy classes with both children and adults, to take into consideration this tacit knowledge, and beliefs and attitudes, together with the informal literacy practices they will have acquired.

Numeracy is a very good example of this. All adults and children have learned by acquisition learning to calculate in their heads. They use different strategies, sometimes those 'caught' from their context, sometimes strategies which they have developed for themselves. Several years ago, it was shown how children in Glasgow who failed their mathematics at school could nevertheless calculate the odds on the races without any visible effort; and non-literate older persons in a rural pub which I visit regularly can calculate threes and fives in dominoes far faster than I can. But such strategies are of relatively limited value and cannot easily be applied to larger and more complex calculations: numeracy (written forms of calculation) is a valuable tool to greater efficiency.

Such practices acquired through acquisition learning over long periods however may be different from (and therefore a potential barrier to) the formalised learning educationalists may wish to pursue with the learners. For example, a recent study provides an example of how in some contexts home-based learning is different from school-based learning. Instead of the Western practice of counting each finger singly (thus using multiples of five and ten), some cultures have taught their children to count by using each joint on each finger, thus giving a value of three to each finger and 15 to each hand (Baker *et al.* 2002; other units such as counting four units to four fingers (base 16) are also known). Using such a calculation strategy could be a powerful tool in the development of multiplication and more complex calculations. To ignore it would not simply be a waste of a resource but could create confusion and a block to learning in the minds of the learner. Teachers need to learn from their students and harness such everyday strategies as they have already developed to their own purposes (Lave 1988; Nunes *et al.* 1993; Saxe 1991). At the same time formalised numeracy learning also needs to learn from the acquisition learning processes involved in learning calculations. It appears that some people in mental calculations subtract in different ways from the formalised way of subtraction. Instead of taking 22 from 30 by subtracting two from zero and carrying figures from one column to another, many people apparently subtract by adding – i.e. by asking 'how many do I need to *add* to 22 to make 30? 22 and 8 make 30. Therefore the answer is 8'. They do not subtract in columns as the formal learning programmes ask them to learn. Again all such learning is done within a context in which words and numbers come together. In everyday learning, there is no such thing as 'five' to be added to 'eight'. There may be five adults and eight children going to the zoo, or five stamps but eight letters. To expect children or adults to learn numeracy from pages of decontextualised and non-verbalised figures is probably not the best medium of instruction. Acquisition learning suggests that numeracy needs to be embedded in words.

A continuum of learning

I want to suggest that there is a continuum of learning, based on this mix of acquisition and formalised learning. At one extreme lie those unintentional and usually accidental learning events which occur continuously as we walk through life. Next comes incidental learning – unconscious learning through acquisition methods which occurs in the course of some other activity: watching television, reading newspapers, talking with other people, engaging in social events, etc. Some will be everyday events (shopping); some more occasional and sometimes even catastrophic (having an accident or bad weather, for example). Then there are various activities in which we are somewhat more conscious of learning, experiential activities arising from immediate life-related concerns, though even here the main focus is still on the task (the so-called 'learning curve' syndrome). Then come more purposeful activities – occasions when we set out to learn something in a more systematic way, using whatever comes to hand for that purpose, but often deliberately disregarding engagement with teachers and formal institutions of learning. Hobbies, the persistent pursuit of interests, make up a large part of this kind of learning. There is an element of conscious learning here – self-controlled and self-evaluated. Further along the continuum lie the self-directed learning projects on which there is so much literature (see Brookfield 1985). It is in this field that the frequently-stated adult autonomous learning takes place: "adults learn what they want to learn and what is meaningful to them" (Illeris 2002b: 20) – a statement made more frequently than it occurs in reality. More formalised and generalised (and consequently less contextualised) forms of learning activities are the distance and open education programmes, where some elements of acquisition learning are often built into the designed learning programme. Towards the further extreme lie those more formalised learning programmes of highly decontextualised learning, using material common to all the learners without paying any regard to their individual preferences, agendas or needs. There are of course no clear boundaries between each of these categories.

Our learning takes place at different points along this continuum. Indeed, any particular learning episode is likely to move along the continuum in one or other direction at various times. It is a dynamic situation, not a case for rigid categories. However, with the exception of unintentional learning, which is often a matter of the transfer of information and the conversion of that information into knowledge, our learning is almost always based on two major elements: acquisition or task-conscious learning (active, imaginative or experimental play, exploration, concrete task performance and self-assessment) and formalised or learning-conscious learning (structured, sequenced, compartmentalised and comprehensive) in different mixes.

The distinctiveness of adult learning?

We can now begin to answer the question we set out at the beginning of this book. Is adult learning different from children's learning? It is the argument of this study that there are two major ways of learning. The first is a natural learning process that we all engage in, unconscious or subconscious; what I have called *task-conscious learning*. The second is a more formalised process of learning; what I have called *learning-conscious learning*. It is also argued that most of our learning activities do or should consist of some form of mixture incorporating elements of both kinds of learning. I suggest that both kinds of learning are common to children, adolescents and adults. The nature of the mix of the two kinds of learning may differ with different groups of learners; but children as well as adults, adults as well as children, engage in both acquisition learning and various forms of more formalised learning.

Wherein then lies the distinctiveness of *adult* learning? Can we define anything which clearly marks off the acquisition and formalised learning of *all* adults from the acquisition and formalised learning of *all* younger persons? What of the various forms of learning which, it has been claimed, are uniquely adult? We can look very briefly at four particular approaches for which adult uniqueness has been claimed, all of which cry out for further research.

First, Mezirow has suggested that the *transformation of meanings* is a uniquely adult form of learning, that children lay down meanings but that adults transform them (Mezirow 2001). I would suggest that we need clearer demonstration that children do not in fact transform meanings or that adults do not create new meanings. Although it is likely that adults do more transformation than children, it is not clear to me that the transformation of meanings is confined to adults alone. We need to look at how children continually transform meanings and learn through so doing. We also need to be careful about being generic about this – to suggest that all adults and all children behave in certain ways at all times.

Secondly, Lave and Wenger (1991) talk about learning through *communities of practice*, by engaging in what they call 'legitimate peripheral participation', striving to engage fully with others so as to enter fully into membership of the chosen group. Again we need to try to determine how far this is uniquely adult. Anecdotal evidence suggests that children too use legitimate peripheral participation, particularly in acquisition learning (gangs, playground groups, computer chatrooms, etc.) but also in more formalised learning situations (classroom coherence, for example). Cohort studies recently examined suggest that this applies to younger persons as well as adults (Imel 2002). Doubts must remain until we have further research.

Thirdly, and perhaps more significantly, there is the field of *experiential learning*. That both children and adults learn through experience is generally acknowledged; and both test new formalised learning against their own prior experience (Draper 1998; Smith and Pourchot 1998), but clearly the experience as well as the lifeworld context of adults are different from those of children. While both have direct engagement with the lifeworld, the constructs they build from that engagement will be different. Adult experience of (for example) money and human relationships is very different from that of children. "An adult's sexual or social experiences are of a kind that mark him [sic] off from the world of children. The same can be said of his experiences of a job, or politics, or war" (Kidd 1973: 46). In particular, adults have had the experience of being a child which a child has not had. Further, the kind of tasks which underlie an adult's task-conscious learning are different from the tasks which children undertake and learn from. Such factors cumulatively would seem to make adult task-conscious and learning-conscious learning different from the learning which children do. Yet on the other hand, children too use experience to test their learning (Merriam 2001; Vaske 2001). The material (experience) on which the learning is based may be different but the learning processes would appear to be the same. Again, we need further research to see how children learn from experience.

Finally, and I confess I find this even more difficult, some have proposed that the person of the adult learner is different. Although the world of lifespan studies (Havighurst 1952; Erikson 1965;

Learning and adults 45

Neugarten 1977) has been shown to be more complex than many have suggested (Hudson 1991), there are those who propose that adulthood consists of a developmental phase in as true a sense as the developmental phases of children and youth; and that therefore an adult is not the same as a child. Brookfield is among the latest to write on this (Brookfield 2000: 89–101). He argues against a concept of 'higher stages' which some of the neo-Piagetian writers suggest (Arlin 1975; Bright 1989; Sutherland 1997: 82–92), but instead suggests that there are four developmental areas in which many if not most adults advance: dialectical thinking (the recognition that specific sites make nonsense of generalised rules and theories), practical logic (the power to make decisions to ignore logical certainties when it is in one's personal interest to do so), what he calls (with more jargon than clarity) epistemic cognition, "becomingly self-consciously aware of their learning styles", and finally critical reflection, acting thinkingly, which he suggests is different from the critical reflection younger persons are capable of (see also Vaske 2001). Others have suggested that adults have developed "domain specific mental schemata …the perception of large meaningful patterns that are not apparent to novices" (Hager 2001: 88 citing Tennant 1991; see also Glaser 1985, Yates and Chandler 1991). This is promising ground but once again (as Brookfield recognises) the research basis for such distinctions is still unsure. I am far from certain that children do not engage in critical reflection, especially in acquisition learning. I am not clear about the stages by which younger persons become conscious of their own learning styles; I wonder when young persons press against the boundaries of regulation whether or not they are engaging in some form of dialectical thinking (in which case very young persons do this); and it is surely possible that children too use practical logic when it is in their interest so to do.

Summary

At this stage of my thinking, then, I wish to suggest that both kinds of learning – task-conscious or acquisition learning and learning-conscious or formalised learning – are common to children, adolescents and adults, although the mix of them may differ from time to time and from learning task to learning task. It may be that it is the mix which needs further research to establish how far adult learning is qualitatively different from the learning which characterises younger persons.

But this leaves us with our second question: if there is little or no difference between adult learning and the learning of younger persons, is there a difference in the 'teaching' of adults, helping adults to learn? It is to this that we must now turn.

Part II

Teaching and adults

In this section, I argue that the uniqueness of adult teaching lies not in the different ways in which adults and children learn, but in the relationships between teacher and learner. These relationships are based on the differing constructs of both parties. The constructs of adult/child and student/teacher will vary, and the range of expectations created by each of these constructs also vary. I draw upon post-colonial concepts of hybridity to suggest that the hybrid of child + student is likely to be very different from that of adult + student, whether held by learner or teacher. It is therefore necessary to understand the way in which such constructs and the hybridities involved are created and the roles implied are fulfilled.

The nature of teaching

The question before us is whether teaching adults is (or should be) different from teaching younger persons, especially children. We have already seen that teaching/education is different from learning, although teaching involves (or is intended to involve) learning. I define teaching as the process of assisting and guiding learning, of promoting and facilitating learning, whether by face-to-face contact or distance/open learning approaches. Most (but not all) of the materials utilised in the process of self-directed learning have been produced with the intention of aiding learning. The implication of this definition is that teaching is always a relationship of some kind. There is someone who occupies the role of 'teacher' (in as wide a sense as I can give it, including matters in the kitchen on occasion, and writers of articles in magazines) and one or more people who occupy the role of learner(s). It is this relationship which I wish to concentrate on in seeking for an answer as to whether teaching adults is different from teaching younger learners, for I argue that we need to understand the various parties involved and the identities they create for themselves if we are to make sense of 'teaching'.

Constructing identities

There is a move today in lifelong learning discussions to break down the barriers between 'education' and other life-related activities, between the classroom and other lifeworld settings. Thus, teaching can be seen as a social activity in much the same way as sports, work, or drinking in pubs are social activities; it is not something of a different nature. Also, as in other social activities, teaching involves constructs and roles, relationships and interaction.

Here we need to draw upon recent understandings of roles and identities which form a key element in modern discussions of education and learning (Kegan 1982; Gates 1991; Bourgeois 2000: 169–70; Gumperz 1982; Marshall 2001: 119–134). To summarise a large and complex field very briefly – a field related to race, gender, sexual orientation, disabilities and abilities, etc. – it can be suggested that recent identity theory points out that the older view of identity as a relatively stable perception of self fixed in youth (Erikson 1968) has now been replaced by a much more fluid picture. Each one of us, it is suggested, lives within a web of social relationships which make up our 'community' and we adopt a set of identities that are carried forward within these networks. The context within which we live is changing very rapidly, and some have suggested that we need a changing or at least flexible identity to cope with these changes. Others affirm that we have many different identities which we use freely to suit our purposes and contexts (see for example, Giddens 1991; Schotter 1993; Gergen 1994; Wintle 1996; Pao *et al.* 1997; Wodak 1999). We are, it is argued, socially constructed from networks of conversations; it is dialogue that promotes and shares our understandings of identities and the roles associated with each identity. None of us is discursively monolithic, but pluralistic and polyphonic (Berger and Luckmann 1966; Fairclough 1992; Gee *et al.* 1996: 209–211).

To agree on the fact that we all construct identities for ourselves and adopt the roles that go with those identities does not require us to accept the extreme post-modernist position in which

> *the search for a true and authentic self and the fulfilment of a pre-given individual autonomy gives way to a playfulness where identity is formed (and 're-formed') by a constantly unfolding desire that is never fully and finally realised... [and in which] the firm ground for the fixed identity becomes a multiple and discontinuous self, traversed by multiple meanings and with shifting identity.*
>
> (Usher *et al.* 1997: 10; see Usher 2000)

In much writing about education and training today, it is becoming more commonly appreciated that persons are "composites of many, often contradictory, self-understandings and identities" (Holland *et al.* 1998: 9) and that educators need "to recognize how the different, changing and multiple identities of individuals impact upon their choices" (Cooke and Kothari 2001: 9; see Grant 1997; Wilson 1999). For both young people and adults, "it is the kinds of informal learning that go on in their everyday lives [that] actually shape their identities" (West 2002). Our identities are changing and being reformulated on the basis of our personality, experience and the context in which we find ourselves. For example, we may interpret the role of parent very differently when facing a teacher of our children in a school-based meeting and when we face those same children in the home.

It is this understanding which stops us from becoming too generic in our approach to adults and to children. Neither child nor adult is generic: they are constructs and such constructs will vary greatly. For we also need to bear in mind that we are not only constructing ourselves but also constructing others; and that we ourselves are being constructed by other people in our various identities and the roles that go with those identities. Almost all of our identities involve relationships; we are children or adults, students or teachers in relation to others who are constructing us as much as we are constructing ourselves and them. There is constant dialogue going on.

Constructing adulthood and childhood

The word 'adult' can be used in several different ways. It can mean a stage in one's life after a predetermined age or ritual. It can represent a status in society, one of acceptance and responsibilities. Used in a sociological context, it will normally refer to a subset of people (adults as against children or adolescents). Or, it may reflect a set of culturally determined ideals and values to be attained as far as possible, ways of behaving. The meaning of the term 'adult' depends on the context within which it is being used. In adult/lifelong education, it carries with it a specific range of meanings.

This being so, we can see that 'adulthood' is a social construct. As UNESCO says (UNESCO 1976), adults are "persons regarded as adult by the society to which they belong." An adult is both self-recognising and recognised by others. This means that the concept of adulthood varies from area to area, from class to class, from culture to culture, from time to time. Perceptions of adulthood will be different in the Ukraine, in the UK and in the USA, although there will be similarities; and beyond this, adulthood in western Europe, in Muslim societies, in Africa and the Far East, in many different indigenous groups and elsewhere, will all be very different.

A number of writers (e.g. Erikson 1978; Knox 1977; Levinson 1986) have explored these fields. Some definitions are clearly inadequate. For example, in one study, an adult "is defined as anyone either age twenty-one or over, married, or the head of a household" (Johnstone and Rivera 1965: 26). On the other hand, another study defines people as "adults because they have assumed responsibility for managing their own lives" (cited in Merriam and Caffarella 1999: 393). Adulthood is often seen as being the "point when individuals may be regarded as having attained a degree of autonomy" (Aspin *et al.* 2001: xvii), although this will rule many adults out of adulthood, not only those with learning difficulties but also those denied autonomy for cultural reasons. Others assert that adulthood is the assumption of certain 'adult' roles in the community: "The taking on of social roles characteristic of adulthood – roles such as worker, spouse or partner, voter, and parent – differentiates adults from children better than chronological age does" (Merriam and Caffarella 1999: 393).

It would seem, however, that in all societies adulthood is established in part by reference to peers and in part by reference to or contrast with childhood. Childhood too is socially constructed (Kessen 1979) and this means that the concept of childhood also varies from culture to culture. In some contexts, childhood constitutes a very short period, in which case adulthood starts 'early'; among other groups, however, childhood is long and adulthood therefore appears to be 'delayed' compared with similar groups in different cultures. For some, childhood is a period of innocence, for others it is an age in which depravity needs to be disciplined (socialised): "Youth cultures are either celebrated as hives of creative industry or attacked as hotbeds of deviancy and delinquency." In some settings, it is believed that children need to be isolated, to be cherished and kept apart from the real world; in other contexts, it is felt that children need to be integrated into the society of which they form a part (Allinson and Prout 1990; Kessen 1979; Wilson 1998).

In Western societies, it can be argued that adulthood is seen to be the antithesis of childhood. There are thus three main characteristics of the construct of adulthood as contrasted with children. First, adults are more mature – that is, they have developed their potential more fully than children have. Secondly, they have more autonomy, more responsibility not only for themselves but also for others:

To say that someone is an adult [in Western societies] is to say that he [sic] is entitled, for example, to a wide-ranging freedom of life-style and to a full participation in the making of social decisions; and it is also to say that he is obliged, among other things, to be mindful of his own deepest interests and to carry a full share of the burdens involved in conducting society and transmitting its benefits. His adulthood consists in his full employment of such rights and his full subjection to such responsibilities.

(Paterson 1979: 10)

Adults are no longer dependent like children, but independent. Thirdly, adults have a greater sense of perspective in relation to themselves. They are not the centre of the world as many children feel themselves to be. They are, on the other hand, not insignificant beings either. They see themselves in a balanced way in their lifeworld and can even be critical of the society of which they are a part.

It can of course be argued that such a concept of adulthood is an ideal. Thus some would urge that we are all engaged in a search for increased autonomy, overcoming the constraining factors of the socio-cultural context in which we live, a search for increasing maturity, the development of our full potential, and a search for increasingly balanced perspectives. These are felt to be part of our idealised sense of adulthood, that to which we strive, that which we encourage in others. The fact that none of us ever achieves our own ideal of adulthood means that our constructs, our dialogue and meaning makings contain an element of idealism. We are only too aware that at times we do not behave as we believe an adult should behave.

However, although such definitions may apply in Western cultures (there is some doubt about their universality even there), they are clearly not appropriate to all groups and cultures. Hungry people have not developed anything like their full maturity or potential. Slum dwellers, slaves and refugees are certainly not autonomous and it is not easy to take a balanced view of life while being a member of an oppressed minority (or even in some cases majority) or under conflict or threat from natural disasters. Yet, in these contexts there are still adults. Thus other cultures see adulthood in different ways from Western cultural values. In many groups in China, for example, rather than autonomy and individual responsibility, adulthood is seen in terms of "family continuity, socially prescribed roles, the acceptance of hierarchical relationships as supreme, compliance with authority, a value on stability versus change ... [it is] an identity that is externally ascribed, subordinated to the collective, seeks fulfilment through the performance of duty ... highly malleable", characterised by "a group-oriented way of thinking [rather than] an individual focus" (Merriam and Caffarella 1999: 129–130, 334; Pratt 1991: 302; Hemphill 1994).

Adulthood, then, is a construct which varies from context to context; and it carries with it varying implications in terms of equality and power. However, beyond the generalised differences between adult and child, we also need to notice that in any society there will be many different concepts of adulthood, not just one. Not only will a child construct an adult differently, but among both children and adults, there will be varying understandings. Concepts of adulthood are changing all the time among the different groups which define adulthood. Being an adult thus will change from group to group and over time. In this changing scene, we also need to note that persons can use more than one concept of adulthood if it suits their particular ambitions and agendas. Studies of indigenous cultures (Aikman 1999; Cajete 1994) suggest that not only do many of these reveal a concept of adulthood (the ideal self) "founded upon traditional tribal values, orientations and principles ... environmental relationships, myths, visionary tradition, traditional arts, tribal community, and nature-centered spirituality" which are missing from most Western constructs of adulthood, but that those who live in such cultures will "simultaneously use the most appropriate concepts, technologies, and content of modern education" to seek to develop their own idealised self (Merriam and Caffarella 1999: 130–1).

The significance of all of this for us as educators of adults is that "there are significant cultural and ideological differences [in how adulthood is defined] ... which must be considered when [developing] educational practices and procedures" (Pratt 1991: 307). For the adults in our learning programmes come in a holistic sense. They bring with themselves (as do children) their own sense of self-identity constructed from various different elements – who they are, what point they have arrived at in their journey towards full adulthood, and how they stand within their own society. This self-identity will affect how they relate to the teacher of adults and also how they learn. We need to learn first how our students regard themselves in terms of their own adulthood and how they construct other adults as well as how we as teachers construct them as adults and as students.

Constructing studenthood

When adults come to adult learning programmes, they also construct themselves as students. Harold Wiltshire noted that education, as distinct from learning, consists of

> ... *planned processes of learning undertaken by intent, the sort of thing that commonly (though not by any means always) goes on in classrooms and that involves some who are teachers and some who are taught ... In much discussion of adult 'education', the word is used much more loosely. Thus in much French writing about* 'education populaire' *it seems to be used so as to include the whole range and apparatus of leisure-time activities — cinemas, libraries, television and sports clubs — on the grounds that these exert an educative influence on people who use them and are therefore aspects of education. Certainly there is a sense in which anything that happens to us, from getting drunk to listening to Beethoven, may be said to be 'quite an education'; and certainly we learn (living tissue can hardly help doing so) from our experiences, including those of our leisure. But such learning is unplanned and largely unintended: we do not go into either the pub or the concert-hall with a primary intention of learning. If we intend to learn we behave differently: we join a class or buy an instruction manual*; we adopt the role of student and submit ourselves to a planned process of tuition.
>
> (Wiltshire in Rogers 1977: 136–7, my emphasis)

Adults, then, when they so need, construct themselves as students.[11]

While there has been a good deal of exploration of the construct of adult and child, less attention has been paid to the various constructs of student, to the identities and roles within such a construct and the discourses involved. Brookfield (2000: 96–100) like one or two others (Rogers 2001; More 1974) has explored a few of the elements which some (not all) adults feel when they construct themselves as students. He suggests that adult students may come to possess a sense that such a role is not really appropriate to their own sense of adulthood, and that it may cut them off from some of their peers (though equally it may create new peers), together with a fear of the risk of failing not just in the eyes of others but also of

---

[11] They do not of course abandon other multiple identities, for example, religious, ethnic, gender, sexual, etc. A Jewish student is still Jewish. But the identity of student *in this context* is to the fore.

themselves. However, we can overgeneralise these elements: there will be a very wide range of highly volatile components involved in each personal construct of what it means to be an adult and a student. Some will be confident, others diffident; some will expect pleasure in learning, others pain. Some will expect adult forms of formalised learning programmes to be like their previous experience of school, others will expect them to be different to school.

However, some general comments may be made in terms of constructs and discourses. Scribner and Cole (1981), for example, note that a learner in a literacy or language class does not simply learn letters, words or grammatical rules. Such a positioning as student "requires the participants to acquire and deploy a particular set of discourses and behaviours" (see Bernstein 1990, 1996), but not just one set of discourses and behaviours: for like the construct of adult, the construct of student too will vary greatly. For some it will be very formal – *in statu pupillari*, under discipline. For others it will be more informal, a lighter hand of guidance being employed to help the normally self-directing learner to develop along certain chosen and, up until now, hidden lines. The persona of 'student' which each participant adopts will be built up from primary and secondary experience, and will be composed of elements of highly individualised and personalised constructs ('what I myself am like in this situation') and also of elements of very generalised constructs (what each of them feels *all* students are like). In most cases, it will tend to clothe itself in the discourse of formalised learning rather than acquisition learning, for they do not see acquisition learning as 'learning' which is the proper activity of a 'student'.

It is this construct of student which helps to account for the range of expectations which both younger and adult students bring with them to the learning situation. There will in addition be the way in which information about the desired learning programme is obtained and held (see Rogers 2002: 9–33), for this too will create expectations. Within the relationship of the teaching–learning situation, it is how the learner positions him/herself as 'student' in relation to the subject matter (Rogers 1993) and to the teacher and the corresponding positioning of the teacher in relation to the student–learner and the subject matter which will determine the effectiveness of the programme.

Although often constructed out of elements of childhood in contemporary society, an adult's construct of studenthood is likely to be wider than and of a different nature from that of a child. Indeed, the key element here is that an adult can draw upon the experience of having been a child but of no longer being a child, whereas the child only has the experience of being a child. Adults tend to be able to see some of the consequences of their learning programme and to expect returns from it which children do not often perceive. Adults have often developed and elaborated on their own self-horizons, perceptions of what they are good at and what they are not good at in learning terms (e.g. "I can't learn languages" – which is plainly false, for all of us have learned at least one language), although children develop self-horizons too quickly. Such learning-related self-horizons do not apply to unconscious acquisition learning or may be expressed in different terms ("I'm no good at mechanical things", or "I'm not artistic," etc.)

Construct of teacher

Further, the construct of student (like adult) is one of relationship – in this case, to a known and accepted 'teacher' and/or to the various texts of the learning situation. Once again, the concept of 'teacher' is a discursive construct. The roles which the student participants expect their chosen or accepted teacher to adopt both as being in authority and 'an' authority (Peters 1966) will be complex and varied, based on prior experience and on culturally accepted norms. It is a question of dialogue – that process in which people "mobilise language by talking, listening and constructing meanings" (Rhodes 2000: 217). A student (even in self-directed learning) is only a student in relation to a teacher and/or to some teaching–learning material. However, the teacher too constructs him/herself as teacher; and just as the construct of adult and child involves relationships (horizontal, with peers; vertical, with non-adults or non-children), so too the construct of teacher involves both horizontal relationships (with other teachers and the equally idealised concept of teacher, just as the concept of adult is idealised) and vertical relationships (with students). The constructs of the teacher as teacher may be very different from the construct which the students have built of the teacher (Rogers 2002: 190–205).

We can see then that teaching consists of a series of relationships between various identities including those of adult-or-child + student and teacher. It is, I suggest, the differences between the relationships built up between the adult + student and teacher and those created between the child + student and teacher which constitute the most important differences between teaching adults and teaching children, not the different ways in which they learn.

Hybridities and agency

Here we may draw upon the recent understandings of hybridity which post-colonial writing has drawn to our attention (e.g. Mohan 2001: 153–167; Goss 1996; Ashcroft *et al.* 1995; Cooke and Kothari 2001: 155–165). Hybridity is moving beyond the dichotomies of self/other, of insider/outsider, of powerless/powerful, etc. There are many different forms of hybrids, unique kinds of mixes like shades of colour. It is not simply a matter of a 'third way' or a simple mixture of the different elements. For hybridity involves agency, power and movement: the hybrid creator uses whatever is felt to be needed in any particular setting to achieve the goals intended. There is here considerable fluidity; hybridity can change when needed, it is not fixed.

I would, however, like to suggest that a child in any learning-conscious learning situation constructs him/herself as both a child and a student (and increasingly in other terms as well); and they construct the teacher in terms of relationship to both the child element and the student element of the hybridity. This is once again a fluid construct, the child often actively constructing themselves in different ways according to their different situations and immediate needs, to achieve their own goals and serve their own perceived interests. The adult too in similar learning-conscious learning situations will construct him/ herself again as a hybrid made up of adult and student; and they will construct the teacher in terms drawn largely from their past experience and cultural perceptions of the 'normal' role of the teacher. I suspect, however, that they normally expect the teacher to relate more to the student part of the hybridity than to the adult part of the hybridity. Much more research is needed into the field of the different constructs of adult and student which adult learners bring to their learning-conscious learning activities, whether self-directed or guided on both sides (student–learner and teacher) and the relationships involved. However, such an analysis suggests that there is a tension in adult lifelong learning programmes which does not exist (or at least does not exist to such a great extent) in children's schooling. In most constructs, the identities and roles of childhood and of studenthood are much more closely related than are the concepts of adulthood and studenthood. The child, for example, perceives both the construct of child and the construct of student in hierarchical terms, in terms of dependency and indeed of control, of some measure of obedience, whereas, the adult construct of that relationship would appear to be much more complex. Some adults will see it in similar terms to the child, for that is the experience they have to draw upon. We have all found adult students who expect to be taught, who want a page of notes, who find discussion between equals a waste of time. For a time and for this purpose, using the agency involved in hybridity, they are constructing themselves as student in a way which will conflict with their own self-construct as adult. They see themselves – in this context – as in need of guidance. They deliberately choose to subordinate their adulthood to a more dependent role as student in order to achieve their purpose. Other adult students however will equally purposefully construct themselves more as adults than as traditional students – more autonomous than children in their control of their own learning, keen and expecting to bring all their experience to the learning situation, to build on rather than deny what they already possess.

Expectations created by identities

Those who teach will also bring with them to the relationship their own constructs of both child/adult and student, as well as their identity as teacher. They too have norms which they expect the learners in learning-conscious situations to conform to. Teachers construct their learners: they expect the children to be both children and students in their own terms. When they come to adult student–learners, there is however a much wider range of constructs employed. Some teachers expect adult students to be more adult than (traditional) student; or they reconstruct the concept of student to be very different from the schooling model. Others expect their learners to abandon their adulthood in large part and temporarily for the purpose of the learning to be achieved.

There is orthodoxy among adult educators that adult students should be treated more as adults than as (traditional) students. It is based upon a series of presuppositions about different motivations, especially motivations for learning. The question of motivation in learning is one which needs re-examination. It applies, of course, only to formalised learning: there can be no question about motivation for learning *per se* for all that unconscious learning which takes place within the performance of some other activity. The motivation in this case is directed towards the task. So, the question turns to whether the motivation of adults to participate in and learn effectively from the many kinds of formalised learning open to them is different from the motivation of children.

The most recent exposition of this position will suffice to describe what many (indeed, perhaps most) adult educators have come to believe. Adults, it is claimed, are different from children when it comes to learning motivation:

> *What we all must realise is that the adult's way of learning is very different from the child's and that adult education must, therefore, be based on quite different premises ... [adults] learn what they want to learn and what is meaningful for them to learn ... [they] are not very inclined to learn something they are not interested in, or in which they cannot see the meaning or importance.*
>
> (Illeris 2002b: 20)

This, it is suggested, is unique to adults because it is part of their construct as adults. There are others however who feel that the same is true for children – that children will only learn what they are interested in (personal interest), what is meaningful (i.e. related to their immediate experience) or what they feel is important for them to learn (for example, in order to pass an examination). They argue that both adults and children can be autonomous, independent and self-directed in their learning (many children pursue individual learning projects as well as adults); and equally both can be the opposite at times.

There is then, within the orthodox view of the adult student, a concept of a particular kind of hybridity of adult + student which many adult educators espouse. This combines the (constructed) autonomy of adulthood with a (constructed) autonomy of learning. The conclusion drawn from this presupposition is clear: "The fundamental requirement is that the adult must take, and must be allowed to take, responsibility for his or her own learning" (Illeris 2002b: 20).

Adulthood as goal

Such a position stresses the adult element in the hybridity of adult + student, so that many adult educators see their education as promoting the adult identities of their learners rather than their identities as student. "A crucial point of all this education is to realise or fulfil the individual to the utmost" (Barrow and Keeney 2001: 53). "The major aim of lifelong education is to promote the autonomy of the individual" (Aspin *et al.* 2001: xxix). In this approach "the Enlightenment notion of the autonomous individual is of paramount importance, for it defines both a goal for and an approach to the practice of adult education" (Marshall 2001: 129). Such views have of course come under attack from several directions including post-modernists (e.g. Luntley 1998). But these drives still remain in much contemporary writing on education. Adult autonomy, for many adult educators in the West, "defines both a goal for and an approach to the practice of adult education" (Usher *et al.* 1997: 94). "A crucial point of... education is to realise or fulfil the individual to the utmost"; "the major aim of lifelong education is to promote the autonomy of the individual" (Aspin *et al.* 2001: xxix). But it would seem that many adult learners do not want this kind of construct. They construct studenthood and adulthood differently and frequently at odds with each other. They prefer to place greater emphasis on the student element as traditionally interpreted.

My argument is that, among many children who are "adopting the role of student and submitting themselves to a planned process of tuition", there is considerable congruity between the perceived roles of both child and student. The aim of both is to become adult. But among adults who similarly "adopt the role of student and submit themselves to a planned process of tuition", there is in many cases a greater incongruity between the traditional role of adulthood as culturally perceived and the traditional role of student as culturally perceived; and that therefore the range of possible hybridities is much wider, some stressing the adult element and some interpreting the student element in terms of dependency and subalternship.

Such possible tensions are felt both by the teacher and the adult student participant. The adult learner may feel the tension between constructing him/herself as both an adult and at the same time as a student; between claiming and exercising their perceived and contextualised rights and responsibilities of adulthood and at the same time claiming and exercising the perceived rights and responsibilities of being a student, however that is constructed (especially claiming and accepting guidance in the learning programme). The teacher may feel these tensions too, for the teacher not only constructs him/herself as adult + teacher (whatever that may mean – and it will mean many different things for different persons), but they will also construct their learners as students. Such constructs will tend to be a mixture of generalised elements ('all teachers/students are like this') and more individualised elements ('this teacher/student has these concerns and that one has different concerns', etc.). Like the student–learners themselves, some teachers will see studenthood in more formalised terms, the application of formalised learning for their student participants, while others will see it in more independent, self-directing terms.

My argument is that in children's education, the perceptions created by both pupil and teacher of the identities and roles of 'student' and 'teacher' will on the whole be very similar, for they rely on the perceived proximity of the identities and roles of both child and student, but among adults there will be a wider range of perceptions. For the adult students, each creating their own hybridity between their concepts of student and adult, the potential for tension will be greater between the hierarchical relationships which are implicit and even explicit in many cultural constructs of student, based as this is largely on childhood paradigms, and the more horizontal relationships inherent in most concepts of adulthood. Thus the relationships implied in most identities of adulthood may contrast markedly with the relationships implied in the identities of students and teachers. At the same time, the perceptions of the teachers on both issues – the adulthood and the studenthood of their student–learners – may differ sharply from those held among the students.

It is this possible incongruity between the various elements of the hybridities created by both students and teachers which accounts for the frequently reported clash between adult students and adult educators over the learning programme. Some adult students wish to be taught in a formalised pattern, surrendering their more horizontal adult constructs in favour of their more hierarchical student constructs. The local demand for formalised learning has been noticed in many adult education contexts: for example, "It is interesting but not surprising that the felt needs of [the learners] commonly relate to courses of the conventional kind" (Wilson 2001: 750). On the other hand, many adult educators wish to provide a more informal open-ended, specifically 'adult' form of teaching–learning programme, drawing upon the experience and all the other inputs which their student participants can provide. On one side is a construct of ignorance and lack of competence; on the other is a valuing of the experience of the participants. The issue centres on power, the teacher often seeking to encourage the student participants to exercise that which in the self-construct of some, if not many, of the student–learners they do not believe they possess.

Conclusion

I have tried to propose that the difference between adult learning programmes and the learning programmes developed for younger persons lies in that part of the teaching–learning processes which concerns relationships rather than in the learning processes themselves.

Mixing acquisition and formalised learning

There is an issue common to the teaching of both children and adults which relates to the particular way in which formalised and acquisition learning are brought together in any learning situation. As we have seen both adults and younger persons use both acquisition (task-conscious) learning and formalised (learning-conscious) learning. Adults' learning programmes and younger persons' learning programmes use formalised learning which may or may not be supplemented as appropriate with acquisition learning; although acquisition learning is going on in any case in both settings. The issue here relates to how far and in what ways acquisition learning can be built more consciously into the formalised learning programme; what kind of mix is involved. There is a real distinction to be drawn between those learning programmes which rely solely on the generalised decontextualised material of formalised learning and those which seek to incorporate the more contextualised and individually purposeful elements of acquisition learning of the student participants. But this is not an adult–younger person distinction. There is a strong case in both kinds of educational and learning programmes for building on and increasing acquisition learning in a mixed learning programme rather than relying on formalised learning alone.

Power in the learning programme

In this respect, then, the learning programmes for adults and children do not differ. Rather the difference between teaching adults and teaching children, I suggest, lies more in the relationships involved – the discourses, the constructs and roles adopted, in the power of the teaching–learning situation. In the education of younger persons, the constructs of both the learners and the teachers of studenthood (acceptance as being under guided learning) are relatively close to their constructs of childhood (as being dependent, under guidance, etc.). In the education of adults, however, the constructs of adulthood, whether created by the teacher or by the student participants, may vary widely, although they will normally (at least in Western cultures) imply some measure of horizontal relationships. These constructs will often differ considerably from the even more widely varying constructs of studenthood which both teacher and student participants adopt, implying some measure of vertical relationships. The power relationships sought by the various participants, both teacher and students, in adult education will normally be very different from those in the education of younger persons.

These two elements – the use of both acquisition learning (contextualised, task-conscious) and formalised learning (decontextualised, learning-conscious), and the more equal power relationships between the teacher and the student learners – come together in the handling of the course itself. There are adult learning programmes which are entirely teacher- or agency-controlled, where both the subject matter and the methods are controlled by the educational institution/ agency and/or the teacher; on the whole, these tend to be generalised learning programmes. There are other programmes which seek to utilise all the various inputs (experience, capacities, insights, etc.) of the individual student participants present in that particular programme rather than rely on the inputs organised and provided by the teacher or agency alone.

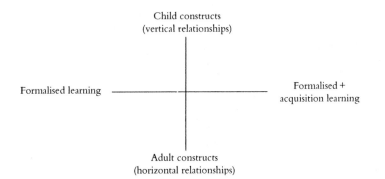

Child constructs
(vertical relationships)

Formalised learning

Formalised +
acquisition learning

Adult constructs
(horizontal relationships)

Start where they are

For me, then, the key distinction between adult learning programmes and those of younger persons does not lie in the difference
between adult learning and children's learning. Rather, it lies in the
contrasting hybrid constructs of adult + student which the participants and the teachers (teacher and student–learners) hold in adult
learning programmes as against the hybrid constructs of child + student which both teacher and student bring to learning programmes
for younger persons. A child confirms his or her childhood by constructing and accepting the role of student. An adult may confirm or
deny his or her identity as an adult by accepting the identity of a
student. There is more likely to be a clash of identities with adult
learners (the phrase in itself may even be felt on occasion to be an
oxymoron) than with younger student learners.

In practice, these two issues (learning and relationships) come
together when we try to explore the consequences of all of this for
our programmes. The policy and practice implications of this analysis, if accepted, will of course need to be worked out in each different situation. However, clearly both the providing agency and the
teacher need to understand the different ways in which the adults
who have come to formalised learning (whether face-to-face, distance or even self-directed) are constructing themselves as both
adults and as students. I would argue that it is a mistake to insist
always on making it "a fundamental requirement that the adult must
take, and must be allowed to take, responsibility for his or how own
learning" (Illeris 2002b: 20) [apart from an inherent hesitation I have
about the word 'must' in any adult education situation!]. Rather than
be normative, ascribing to all adult students characteristics we would
like them to have rather than as they really are, I would prefer to start
where my students are, with what they wish to do, with the ways in
which they have constructed themselves as adults and as students.
If some adults wish to construct themselves as students in terms of
being subaltern, and to construct the role of teacher as being
dominant, to use formalised learning only in the programme, then
I would wish to accept that role, at least for a time. I too have my
own constructs of adult and of student which suggest to me that I
might try to encourage them to become more self-directing and

autonomous. I do not wish to have their constructs imposed on me, but even more importantly I do not wish to impose my constructs on them.

We can then start with their own acquisition and task-conscious learning and to help them to make that more conscious, more structured, related to general principles. Alternatively, we can start with the more generalised learning-conscious programme and to seek to bring more and more task-conscious learning into the formalised learning situation. I believe that it is possible to draw up a learning programme which combines the experience of each of the learners (individualised, concrete and personally constructed) and the generalised principles relating to the learning programme, to enable the learning to be usable in more than one context. But the determining factor should, in my opinion, be the expectations of the student participants rather than the preferences of the teacher or the educational institution. Some will wish to use their own experience immediately; others will expect a more formalised approach. Whether one starts with the concrete, immediate and task-conscious learning or with the more generalised decontextualised formalised learning will depend on the situation concerned. Institutionalised learning programmes will, on the whole, tend to start working in a formalised way and many students in such a situation will desire a formalised learning programme; but it is possible, gradually, to encourage them to engage in more and more task-conscious learning, using their own experience for that purpose. In that way, they are likely to come to increase their own control over their own learning, but that is very different from insisting that they *must* take responsibility for their own learning from the start.

I repeat what I said many years ago (Rogers 1986: 68–71): as teachers of adults, we must understand the different ways in which our adult students are already learning outside the classroom. This is the most important part of learning but also the most neglected. We can then introduce elements of that learning into our formalised learning programmes or indeed build our learning programmes on to that experience of learning they already have. What I have come to appreciate in greater detail since that was first written is that we also need to understand how our adult students are constructing themselves both as adults and as students, and we should also become aware of just how we as teachers are constructing our students both as adults and as students. The gap between these two sets of constructs may be what makes teaching adults different from teaching children.

References

Abrahams D and Hogg M (eds) (1990) *Social Identity Theory: Constructive and Critical Advances*. London: Harvester Wheatsheaf.

Aikman S (1999) *Intercultural Education and Literacy*. Amsterdam: Benjamin.

Allinson J and Prout J (1990) *Constructing and Reconstructing Childhood*. Basingstoke: Falmer Press.

Argyris C (1993) *Knowledge for Action*. San Francisco: Jossey Bass.

Argyris C and Schon DA (1974) *Theory in Practice: Increasing Professional Effectiveness*. San Francisco: Jossey Bass.

Argyris C and Schon DA (1978) *Organizational Learning: A Theory of Action Perspective*. Reading, MA: Addison-Wesley.

Arlin PK (1975) Cognitive development in adulthood: a fifth stage? *Developmental Psychology* **11**: 602–606.

Ashcroft B, Griffiths G and Tiffin H (eds) (1995) *Post-Colonial Studies Reader*. London: Routledge.

Aspin D and Chapman J (2001) Towards a philosophy of lifelong learning. In: D Aspin *et al.* (eds) *International Handbook of Lifelong Learning*, pp. 3–34. London: Kluwer Academic Publishers.

Aspin D, Chapman J, Hatton M and Sawano Y (eds) (2001) *International Handbook of Lifelong Learning*. London: Kluwer Academic Publishers.

Bagnall R (2001) Locating lifelong learning and education in contemporary currents of thought and culture. In: D Aspin *et al.* (eds) *International Handbook of Lifelong Learning*, pp. 35–52. London: Kluwer Academic Publishers.

Baker D, Street BV and Tomlin A (2002) *Counting in Contexts: Understanding Relationships Between Home and School Numeracy Practices*, unpublished paper.

Barrow R and Keeney P (2001) Lifelong learning and personal fulfilment. In: D Aspin *et al.* (eds) *International Handbook of Lifelong Learning*, pp. 53–60. London: Kluwer Academic Publishers.

Bateson G (1973) *Steps to an Ecology of Mind*. London: Paladin.

Beard R (1976) *Teaching and Learning in Higher Education*, 3rd edn. Harmondsworth: Penguin.

Berger P and Luckmann T (1966) *Social Construction of Reality*. New York: Anchor.

Bernstein B (1975) *Class Codes and Control: Towards a Theory of Educational Transmissions*. London: Routledge and Kegan Paul.

Bernstein B (1990) *The Structuring of Pedagogic Discourse*. London: Routledge.

Bernstein B (1996) *Pedagogy, Symbolic Control and Identity*. London: Taylor & Francis.

Birren JE and Schaie KW (eds) (1996) *Handbook of the Psychology of Aging*. Orlando, FL: Academic Press.

Bjorklund DF, Schneider W and Blasi CH (2003) Memory. In: L Nadel (ed.) *Encyclopedia of Cognitive Science*, vol. 2, pp. 1059–1065. London: Nature Publishing Group.

Bjornavold J (2000) *Making Learning Visible: Identification, Assessment and Recognition of Non-formal Learning*. Thesaloniki: CEDEFOP.

Bloome D, Puro P and Theoduro E (1989) Procedural display and classroom lessons. *Curriculum Inquiry* **19**(3): 265–291.

Boud D, Cohen R and Sampson J (2001) *Peer Learning in Higher Education: Learning From and With Each Other*. London: Kogan Page.

Boud D, Cohen R and Walker D (eds) (1993) *Using Experience for Learning*. Buckingham: Open University Press.

Bourgeois E (2000) Sociocultural mobility: language learning and identity. In: A Bron and M Schemmann (eds) *Language, Mobility, Identity*, Bochum Studies in International Adult Education, pp. 163–184. Hamburg: LIT Verlag.

Breier M, Taetsane M and Sait L (1996) Reading and writing in the taxi industry. In: M Prinsloo and M Breier (eds) *Social Uses of Literacy*. Amsterdam: Benjamins.

Bright B (1989) *Theory and Practice in the Study of Adult Education: The Epistemological Debate*. London: Routledge.

Bron A and Schemmann M (eds) (2000) *Language, Mobility, Identity*, Bochum Studies in International Adult Education. Hamburg: LIT Verlag.

Brookfield SD (2000) Adult cognition as a dimension of lifelong learning. In: J Field and M Leicester (eds) *Lifelong Learning: Education Across the Lifespan*. London: Routledge.

Brookfield SD (ed.) (1985) *Self-Directed Learning: From Theory to Practice*. San Francisco: Jossey Bass.

Brown (1990) *International Encyclopedia of Education*. Cited in Bjornavold (2000), pp. 204.

Bruner J (1983) *In Search of Mind: Essays in Autobiography*. New York: Harper and Row.

Cairns T (2001) Acquiring basic skills as part of everyday life. *Adults Learning* **13**(3): 20–22.

Cajete G (1994) *Look to the Mountain: An Ecology of Indigenous Education*. Amsterdam: North-Holland.

Cenoz J and Genesee F (eds) (2001) *Trends in Bilingual Acquisition*. Amsterdam: Benjamin.

Chapman J and Aspin D (2001) Schools and the learning community: laying the basis for learning across the lifespan. In: D Aspin *et al.* (eds) *International Handbook of Lifelong Learning*, pp. 405–446. London: Kluwer Academic Publishers.

Cleeremans A (2003) Implicit learning models. In: L Nadel (ed.) *Encyclopedia of Cognitive Science*, vol. 2, pp. 491–499. London: Nature Publishing Group.

Coben D (1998) *Radical Heroes: Gramsci, Freire and the Politics of Adult Education*. Boulder, CO: Garland.

Coffield F (ed.) (2000) *The Necessity of Informal Learning*. Bristol: Policy Press.

Cohen J and Leicester M (2000) The evolution of the learning society: brain science, social science and lifelong learning. In: J Field and M Leicester (eds) *Lifelong Learning: Education Across the Lifespan*. London: Routledge.

Cohen N (1998) *Learning to Return: Learning in Preparation for the Return of Refugees from Mexico to Guatemala*. Reading, UK: Education for Development.

Cole M and Scribner S (1974) *Culture and Thought*. New York: Wiley.

Cook SDN and Yanow D (1993) Culture and organizational learning. *Journal of Management Enquiry* **2**: 373–390.

Cooke B and Kothari U (eds) (2001) *Participation: The New Tyranny?* London: Zed Books.

Courtney S, Vasa S, Luo J and Muggy V (1999) Characteristics of Adults as Learners and Implications for Computer-Based Systems for Information and Instruction, ED 451 340, cited in Kerka (2002).

Dave R (ed.) (1976) *Foundations of Lifelong Education*. Oxford: Pergamon.

Dewey J (1916) *Democracy and Education*. New York: Collier Macmillan.

Dewey J (1971) *The Early Works of John Dewey 1882–1898* vol. V, *Pedagogic Creed*. London: Feffer and Simons.

Dixon NM (1999) *The Organizational Learning Cycle: How We Can Learn Collectively*. London: Gower.

Dore R (1976) *The Diploma Disease*. London: Allen and Unwin.

Draper JA (1998) The Metamorphoses of 'Andragogy'. *Canadian Journal for the Study of Adult Education* **12**(1): 3–26.

Duke C (2001) Lifelong learning and tertiary education: the learning university revisited. In: D Aspin *et al.* (eds) *International Handbook of Lifelong Learning*, pp. 501–528. London: Kluwer Academic Publishers.

Edwards R (2000) Lifelong learning, lifelong learning, lifelong learning: a recurrent education? In: J Field and M Leicester (eds) *Lifelong Learning: Education Across the Lifespan*, pp. 3–11. London: Routledge.

Elsdon KT, Reynolds J and Stewart S (1995) *Voluntary Organisations: Citizenship, Learning and Change*. Leicester, UK: NIACE.

Encyclopedia of Informal Education. At: http://www.infed.org/lifelonglearning/b-aeprint.htm

Engstrom Y (1987) *Learning by Expanding: An Activity–Theoretical Approach to Developmental Research.* Helsinki: Orientakonsultit.

Engstrom Y (1994) *Training for Change: A New Approach to Instruction and Learning in Working Life.* Geneva: ILO.

Engstrom Y, Miettimen R and Punamaki RL (eds) (1999) *Perspectives on Activity Theory.* Cambridge, UK: Cambridge University Press.

Enslin P, Pendlebury S and Tjattas M (2001) Political inclusion, democratic empowerment and lifelong learning. In: D Aspin *et al.* (eds) *International Handbook of Lifelong Learning*, pp. 61–78. London: Kluwer Academic Publishers.

Eraut M (2000) Non-formal learning, implicit learning, and tacit knowledge in professional work. In: F Coffield (ed.) *The Necessity of Informal Learning.* Bristol: Policy Press.

Erikson EH (1965) *Childhood and Society.* Harmondsworth: Penguin.

Erikson EH (1968) *Identity, Youth and Crisis.* New York: Norton.

Erikson EH (1978) *Adulthood.* New York: Norton.

Evans N (1987) Assessing *Experiential Learning.* London: Longman.

Evans N (1992) *Experiential Learning: Assessment and Accreditation.* London: Routledge.

Fairclough N (1992) *Discourse and Social Change.* Cambridge: Polity Press.

Faure E *et al.* (1972) *Learning To Be: The World of Education Today and Tomorrow.* Paris: UNESCO.

Felman S (1982) Psychoanalysis and education: teaching terminable and interminable. *Yale French Studies* **63**: 21–41, cited in Visser (2001).

Field J and Leicester M (eds) (2000) *Lifelong Learning: Education Across the Lifespan.* London: Routledge.

Foley G (1999) *Learning in Social Action: A Contribution to Understanding Informal Education.* London: Zed Books.

Freire P (1972) *Pedagogy of the Oppressed.* Harmondsworth: Penguin.

Garrick J and Rhodes C (eds) (2000) *Research and Knowledge at Work.* London: Routledge.

Gates H (1991) Critical Fanonism. *Critical Inquiry* **17**: 457–470.

Gee JP (2003) *What Video Games Have to Teach Us About Learning and Literacy.* New York: Palgrave/St Martin's.

Gee JP, Hull G and Lankshear C (1996) *The New Work Order: Behind the Language of the New Capitalism.* Boulder, CO: Westview Press.

Gergen KJ (1994) *Reality and Relationships.* Cambridge MA: Harvard University Press.

Giddens A (1991) *Modernity and Self-Identity*. Cambridge, UK: Polity Press.

Glaser R (1985) *The Nature of Expertise*. Columbus, OH: ERIC.

Goss J (1996) Post-colonialism: subverting whose empire? *Third World Quarterly* **17**(1): 239–250.

Grant N (1997) Some problems of identity and education: a comparative examination of multicultural education. *Comparative Education* **33**(1): 9–28.

Griffey S and Kelleher M (1996) How do people learn? Connecting practice with theory. *Training Matters* **5**: 3–9.

Guile D and Young M (2001) Apprenticeship as a conceptual basis for a social theory of learning. In: Paechter C, Preedy M, Scott D and Soler J (ed.) *Knowledge, Power and Learning*, pp. 56–73. London: Paul Chapman and Open University.

Gumperz G (ed.) 1982 *Language and Social Identity*. Cambridge, UK: Cambridge University Press.

Gustavsson B (1997) Lifelong learning reconsidered. In: S Walters (ed.) *Globalization, Adult Education and Training: Impacts and Issues*, pp. 237–249. London: Zed Books.

Habermas J (1972) *Knowledge and Human Interests*. London: Heinemann.

Hager P (2001) Lifelong learning and the contribution of informal learning. In: D Aspin *et al.* (eds) *International Handbook of Lifelong Learning*, pp. 79–92. London: Kluwer Academic Publishers.

Hanna W and Haillet P (2001) Lifelong learning and the private sector. In: D Aspin *et al.* (eds) *International Handbook of Lifelong Learning*, pp. 681–694. London: Kluwer Academic Publishers.

Hannah J (2000) Education, training and adult refugees in the UK and Australia. In: J Field and M Leicester (eds) *Lifelong Learning: Education Across the Lifespan*, pp. 263–275. London: Routledge.

Hatch E (ed.) (1978) *Second Language Acquisition*. Rowley, MA: Newbury House.

Havighurst RJ (1952) *Developmental Tasks and Education*. New York: McKay (third edn 1972).

Heath SB (1983) *Ways with Words*. Cambridge, UK: Cambridge University Press.

Hemphill DF (1994) Critical Rationality from a Cross-cultural Perspective. *Proceedings of Adult Education Research Conference*. Knoxville, Tennessee: University of Tennessee.

Henry M, Lingard B, Rizvi F and Taylor S (2001) *The OECD, Globalisation and Education Policy*. Oxford: Pergamon.

Holland D, Lachicotte J, Skinner D and Cain C (1998) *Identity and Agency in Cultural Worlds*. Cambridge, MA: Harvard University Press.

Honey P and Mumford A (1986) *Manual of Learning Styles*. London: Peter Honey.

Houle CO (1961) *The Inquiring Mind: A Study of the Adults who Continue to Learn*. Madison, WI: University of Wisconsin Press.

Hudson F (1991) *The Adult Years*. San Francisco: Jossey Bass.

Illeris K (ed.) (2000) *Adult Education in the Perspective of the Learners*. Copenhagen: Roskilde.

Illeris K (2002a) *The Three Dimensions of Learning*. Roskilde: Roskilde University Press.

Illeris K (2002b) Understanding the conditions of adult learning. *Adults Learning* **14**(4): 18–20.

Imel S (2002) *Adult Learning in Cohort Groups*. Columbus, Ohio: ERIC.

Istance D, Schvetze HG and Schuller T (eds) (2002) *International Perspectives on Lifelong Learning: From Recurrent Education to the Knowledge Society*. Buckingham: Open University Press.

Jarvis P (1987) *Adult Learning in the Social Context*. London: Croom Helm.

Jarvis P (1995) *Adult and Continuing Education: Theory and Practice*, 2nd edn. London: Routledge.

Jarvis P (2000) The corporate university, in J Field and M Leicester (eds) *Lifelong Learning: Education Across the Lifespan*, pp. 43–55. London: Routledge.

Jarvis P, Holford J and Griffin C (1998) *Theory and Practice of Learning*. London: Kogan Page.

Johnstone JWC and Rivera RJ (1965) *Volunteers for Learning: A Study of the Educational Pursuits of Adults*. Hawthorne, NY: Aldine Press.

Kegan R (1982) *The Evolving Self*. Cambridge, MA: Harvard University Press.

Kerka S (2002) Teaching adults: is it different? *Myths and Realties 21*, Columbus, Ohio: ERIC.

Kessel FS, Bornstein MH and Sameroff AJ (eds) (1991) *Contemporary Constructions of the Child: Essays in Honour of William Kessen*. Hillsdale, NJ: Lawrence Erlbaum Associates.

Kessen W (1979) American children and other cultural inventions. *American Psychologist* **34**: 815–820.

Kidd JB (2002) Knowledge creation in Japanese manufacturing companies in Italy: reflections upon organizational learning. In: F Reeve, M Cartwright and R Edwards (eds) *Supporting Lifelong Learning, vol. 2: Organizing Learning*, pp. 109–126. London: Routledge/Falmer.

Kidd JR (1973) *How Adults Learn*. New York: Association Press.

Kirpal P (1976) Historical studies and the foundation of lifelong education. In: R Dave (ed.) *Foundations of Lifelong Learning*. Oxford: Pergamon.

Knox AB (1977) *Adult Development and Learning*. San Francisco: Jossey Bass.

Kolb DA (1976) *Learning Style Inventory Technical Manual*. Boston, MA: McBer.

Kolb DA (1984) *Experiential Learning: Experience as the Source of Learning and Development*. Englefield Cliffs, NJ: Prentice Hall.

Kozlowski SWJ (1995) Organizational change, informal learning and adaptation: emerging trends in training and continuing education. *Journal of Continuing Higher Education* **43**(1): 2–11.

Krashen SD (1982) *Principles and Practice in Second Language Acquisition*. Oxford: Pergamon.

Lave J (1988) *Cognition in Practice: Mind, Maths and Culture in Everyday Life*. Cambridge, UK: Cambridge University Press.

Lave J and Wenger E (1991) *Situated Learning: Legitimate Peripheral Participation*. Cambridge, UK: Cambridge University Press.

Levinson DJ (1986) A conception of adult development. *American Psychologist* **41**(1): 3–13.

Lewin K and Grabbe P (1945) Conduct, knowledge and acceptance of new values. *Journal of Social Issues* **1**(3).

Llorente JC and Coben D (2003) Reconstituting our understanding of the relationship between knowledge and power in analysis of the education of adults: socio-cognitive and political dimensions. *Compare* **33**(1): 101–113.

Longworth N and Davies WK (1996) *Lifelong Learning*. London: Kogan Page.

Lucas AM (1983) Scientific literacy and informal learning. *Studies in Science Education* **10**: 1–36.

Luntley M (1998) *Reason, Truth and Self: the Post-modern Reconditioned*. London: Routledge.

Marshall James (2001) Caring for the self. In: D Aspin *et al.* (eds) *International Handbook of Lifelong Learning*, pp. 119–134. London: Kluwer Academic Publishers.

Marsick V and Watkins K (1990) *Informal and Incidental Learning in the Workplace*. London: Routledge.

McGivney V (1999) *Informal Learning in the Community*. Leicester: NIACE.

Merriam S and Caffarella R (1999) *Learning in Adulthood*. San Francisco: Jossey Bass.

Merriam SB (2001) Andragogy and self-directed learning. In: SB Merriam (ed.) *New Update on Adult Learning Theory: New Directions for Adult and Continuing Education*, pp. 3–13. San Francisco: Jossey Bass.

Mezirow *et al.* (2001) *Learning as Transformation*. San Francisco: Jossey Bass.

Miller ME and Cook-Greuter SR (eds) (1994) *Transcendence and Mature Adult Thought in Adulthood: The Further Reaches of Adult Development*. London: Rowman and Littlefield.

Mohan G (2001) Beyond participation: strategies for deeper empowerment. In: Cooke and Kothari (eds) *Participation: The New Tyranny?*, pp. 153–167. London: Zed Books.

More WS (1974) *Emotions and Adult Learning*. Farnborough, UK: Saxon House.

Mulligan NW (2003) Memory: implicit and explicit. In: L Nadel (ed.) *Encyclopedia of Cognitive Science*, vol. 2, pp. 1114–1120. London: Nature Publishing Group.

Neugarten BL (1977) Personality and aging. In: JE Birren and KW Scaie (eds) *Handbook of the Psychology of Aging*. New York: van Nostrand Reinhold.

Nonaka I (1994) A dynamic theory of organizational knowledge creation. *Organizational Science* 5(1): 14–37.

Nonaka I and Takeuchi H (1995) *The Knowledge-creating Company*. Oxford: Oxford University Press.

Nowlen PM (1988) *New Approach to Continuing Education in Business and the Professions: The Performance Model*. London: Macmillan.

Nunes T, Scliemann A and Carraher D (1993) *Street Maths and School Maths*. Cambridge, UK: Cambridge University Press.

Pao DL, Wong SD and Teuben-Rowe S (1997) Identity formation for mixed-heritage adults and implications for educators. *TESOL Quarterly* 3: 622–631.

Paterson KW (1979) *Values, Education and the Adult*. London: Routledge.

Peters JM et al. (1991) *Adult Education: Evolution and Achievements in a Developing Field of Study*. San Francisco: Jossey Bass.

Peters RS (1966) *Ethics and Education*. London: Allen and Unwin.

Phillips DC (1995) The good, the bad and the ugly: the many faces of constructivism. *Educational Researcher* 24(7): 5–12.

Polyani M (1966) *The Tacit Dimension*. New York: Doubleday.

Pratt DD (1991) Conceptions of the self in China and the US: contrasting foundations for adult development. *International Journal of Intercultural Relations* 15(3): 285–310.

Rahman A (1993) *People's Self-Development: Perspectives on Participatory Action Research*. London: Zed Books.

Reber AS (2003) Implicit learning. In: L Nadel (ed.) *Encyclopedia of Cognitive Science*, vol. 2, pp. 481–491 London: Nature Publishing Group.

Reeve F, Cartwright M, Edwards R (eds) (2002) *Supporting Lifelong Learning*, vol. 2: *Organizing Learning*. London: Routledge/Falmer.

Reingold EM and Ray CA (2003) Implicit cognition. In: L Nadel (ed.) *Encyclopedia of Cognitive Science*, vol. 2, pp. 481–5. London: Nature Publishing Group.

Reischemann J (1986) *Learning en passant*. Unpublished paper, cited in Jarvis (1995), pp. 72.

Resnick L (1987) Learning in school and out. *Educational Researcher* **16**(9): 13–20.

Revans R (1980) *The ABC of Action Learning.* London: Lemas and Crane.

Rhodes C (2000) 'Doing' knowledge at work: dialogue, monologue and power in organisational learning. In: J Garrick and C Rhodes (eds) *Research and Knowledge at Work*, pp. 217–231. London: Routledge.

Richardson LD and Wolfe M (2001) *Principles and Practice of Informal Education.* London: Routledge.

Rogers A (ed.) (1977) *The Spirit and the Form: Essays By and In Honour of Harold Wiltshire.* Nottingham: University of Nottingham.

Rogers A (1986) *Teaching Adults* (1st edn). Buckingham: Open University Press.

Rogers A (1993) Adult learning maps and the teaching process. *Studies in the Education of Adults* **22**(2): 199–220.

Rogers A (1996) *Teaching Adults*, 2nd edn. Buckingham: Open University Press.

Rogers A (1997) Learning: can we change the discourse? *Adults Learning* **8**(5): 116–117.

Rogers A (2002) *Teaching Adults* (3rd edn). Buckingham: Open University Press.

Rogers A (forthcoming) *Non-formal Education: Flexible Schooling or Participatory Education?*

Rogers CR (1974) *On Becoming a Person.* Boston, MA: Houghton Mifflin.

Rogers J (2001) *Adults Learning.* Buckingham: Open University Press.

Rogoff B and Lave J (1984) *Everyday Cognition: Its Development in Social Context.* Cambridge, MA: Harvard University Press.

Rorty R (1979) *Philosophy and the Mirror of Nature.* Princeton, NJ: Princeton University Press.

Ryle G (1949) *The Concept of Mind.* London: Hutchinson.

Sallis E and Jones G (2002) *Knowledge Management in Education: Enhancing Learning and Education.* London: Kogan Page.

Saxe J (1991) *Culture and Cognitive Development: Studies in Mathematical Understanding.* London: LEA Publishers.

Schaie KW (1996) Intellectual development in adulthood. In: JE Birren and KW Schaie (eds) *Handbook of the Psychology of Aging.* Orlando, FL: Academic Press.

Schon DA (1983) *The Reflective Practitioner: How Professionals Think in Action.* New York: Basic Books.

Schon DA (1995) *Educating the Reflective Practitioner.* San Francisco: Jossey Bass.

Schotter J (1993) *Cultural Politics of Everyday Life.* Buckingham: Open University Press.

Scott SM (1996) Conscientization as the object of practice, *Proceedings of the 37th Annual Adult Education Research Conference*. Tampa, FL: University of South Florida Press.

Scribner S (1988) *Head and Hand: An Action Approach to Thinking*. Columbus, OH: ERIC.

Scribner S and Cole M (1981) *The Psychology of Literacy*. Cambridge, MA: Harvard University Press.

Scribner S, DiBello L, Kindred J and Zazanis E (1991) *Co-ordinating Two Knowledge Systems: A Case Study*. New York: City University of New York.

Simonsen B (2000) New young people, new forms of consciousness, new educational methods. In: K Illeris (ed.) *Adult Education in the Perspective of the Learners*. Copenhagen: Roskilde.

Smith J and Spurling A (1999) *Lifelong Learning: Riding the Tiger*. London: Cassell.

Smith MC and Pourchot T (eds) (1998) *Adult Learning and Development: Perspectives from Educational Psychology*. Mahwah, NJ: Erlbaum.

Smith RM (1982) *Learning How to Learn: Applied Learning Theory for Adults*. Chicago: Follett.

Snook I (2001) Lifelong education: some Deweyian themes. In: D Aspin et al. (eds) *International Handbook of Lifelong Learning*, pp. 155–164. London: Kluwer Academic Publishers.

St Clair R (2002) *Andragogy Revisited: Theory for the Twenty-first Century? Myths and Realities 19*. Columbus, OH: ERIC.

Steedman H, Gospel H and Ryan P (1998) *Apprenticeship: A Strategy for Growth*. London: LSE Centre for Economic Performance.

Steffe LP and Gale J (eds) (1995) *Constructivism in Education*. Hillsdale, NJ: Lawrence Erlbaum Associates.

Sutherland P (1997) *Adult Learning: A Reader*. London: Kogan Page.

Tennant MC (1991) The psychology of adult teaching and learning. In: JM Peters et al. (eds) *Education: Evolution and Achievements in a Developing Field of Study*. San Francisco: Jossey Bass.

Thomas LE (1994) Cognitive development and transcendence: an emerging transpersonal paradigm of consciousness. In: ME Miller and SR Cook-Greuter (eds) *Transcendence and Mature Adult Thought in Adulthood: The Further Reaches of Adult Development*. London: Rowman and Littlefield.

Tice ET (1997) Educating adults: a matter of balance. *Adults Learning* **9**(1): 18–21.

Tough M (1979) *The Adult's Learning Projects*, 2nd edn. Toronto: OISE.

UNESCO (1976) *Nairobi: Recommendations on the Development of Adult Education: Declaration of Nairobi Conference*. Paris: UNESCO.

Usher R (1993) Experiential learning or learning from experience: does it make a difference? In: D Boud, R Cohen and D Walker (eds) *Using Experience for Learning*. Buckingham: Open University Press.

Usher R (2000) Impossible identities, unstable boundaries: managing experience differently. In: K Illeris (ed.) *Adult Education in the Perspective of the Learners*. Copenhagen: Roskilde.

Usher R (2001) Lifelong learning in the postmodern. In: D Aspin *et al.* (eds) *International Handbook of Lifelong Learning*, pp. 165–182. London: Kluwer Academic Publishers.

Usher R, Bryant I and Johnston R (1997) *Adult Education and the Post-Modern Challenge: Learning Beyond the Limits*. London: Routledge.

Vaske JM (2001) *Critical Thinking in Adult Education: An Elusive Quest for a Definition of the Field*. Ed D thesis, Drake University, Iowa, USA, cited in Kerka (2002).

Visser J (2001) Integrity, completeness and comprehensiveness of the learning environment: meeting the basic learning needs of all throughout life. In: D Aspin *et al.* (eds) *International Handbook of Lifelong Learning*, pp. 473–500. London: Kluwer Academic Publishers.

Vygotsky LS (1996 edn) *Thought and Language*. Cambridge, MA: MIT Press.

Walker J (2001) Lifelong learning and the learning organization. In: D Aspin *et al.* (eds) *International Handbook of Lifelong Learning*, pp. 619–644. London: Kluwer Academic Publishers.

Walters S (ed.) (1997) *Globalization, Adult Education and Training: Impacts and Issues*. London: Zed Books.

Wertsch JV (1985) *Vygotsky and the Social Formation of Mind*. Cambridge, MA: Harvard University Press.

Wertsch JV (1991) *Voices of the Mind: A Socio-cultural Approach to Mediated Practice*. London: Harvester Wheatsheaf.

West L (2002) *Glimpses Across the Divide: A Study of the Community Arts Among Disaffected Young Men and Women in East London*. London: University of East London.

Wilber K (1982) *A Sociable God*. New York: McGraw-Hill.

Wilber K (1983) *Eye to Eye*. New York: Doubleday.

Wilson AL (1999) Creating identities of dependency: adult education as a knowledge-power regime. *International Journal of Lifelong Education* **18**(2): 85–93.

Wilson J (2001) Lifelong learning, the individual and community self-help. In: D Aspin *et al.* (eds) *International Handbook of Lifelong Learning*, pp. 733–754. London: Kluwer Academic Publishers.

Wilson S (1998) *Social and Cultural History of Personal Naming in Western Europe*. London: University College Press.

Wintle M (ed.) (1996) *Culture and Identity in Europe: Perceptions of Divergence and Unity in Past and Present.* Aldershot, Brookfield, USA: Avebury/ Ashgate Publishing Company.

Wodak E (1999) *The Discursive Construction of National Identity.* Edinburgh: Edinburgh University Press.

Yates G and Chandler M (1991) The cognitive psychology of knowledge: basic research findings and educational implications. *Australian Journal of Education* **35**(2): 131–153.

Index

JOURNALS AVAILABLE FROM NIACE

Studies in the Education of Adults
Published twice a year
ISSN 0266-0830
Online version ISSN 1478-9833

Studies in the Education of Adults is an international, refereed journal. It publishes theoretical, empirical and historical studies from all sectors of post-initial education and training and provides a forum for debate and development of key concepts. The journal recognises the importance of theory in academic debate, supports innovative work which challenges conventional wisdom, and seeks to ensure a diversity of voices and paradigms.

'In this journal the frontiers of disciplined inquiry collide with the everyday realities of adult learning, work, culture and politics to produce sound practical insights and new intellectual achievements.'

(Arthur L Wilson, Cornell University, co-editor of *Adult Education Quarterly*)

Journal of Access Policy and Practice
Published twice a year
ISSN 1740-1348
Online version ISSN 1740-1356

The *Journal of Access Policy and Practice* informs and supports development in access and widening participation. It explores education policy and practice as it affects access to learning and surveys the field, both nationally and internationally. Informed by theory and current research the journal shares ideas and practical solutions to create wider and deeper participation in lifelong learning and offers a space for practitioners and academics to critically reflect and debate different perspectives.

Journal of Adult & Continuing Education

Published twice a year
ISSN 1477-9714
Online version ISSN 1477-9714

This is a comprehensive international refereed journal covering aspects of theory and practice in adult and continuing education. Published twice a year it provides a forum for rigorous theoretical and empirical work in the broad fields of adult, community and continuing education. It is available to subscribers electronically.

'*Hitting the right pitch between critical analysis and practicality is not an easy task and yet I suspect that this is what most adult educators are looking for in a publication. JACE is certainly aimed at achieving this difficult combination of analysis and relevance and deserves a wide audience for its end product.*'

(John Benseman, University of Auckland, co-editor of the *New Zealand Journal of Adult Learning*)

For full details of these journals and all NIACE publications, visit the NIACE website at www.niace.org.uk/publications

These journals are available from:

NIACE Subscriptions
Renaissance House
20 Princess Road West
Leicester LE1 6TP

Tel: +44 (0)116 204 4215